THE

ELEMENTS OF CHARACTER.

BY

MARY G. CHANDLER.

"An exclusively intellectual education leads, by a very obvious process, to hard-heartedness and the contempt of all moral influences. An exclusively moral education tends to fatuity by the over-excitement of the sensibilities. An exclusively religious education ends in insanity, if it do not take a directly opposite course and lead to atheism."

—EDINBURGH REVIEW.

THE REV. E.H. SEARS, MY FORMER PASTOR,
UNDER WHOSE SPIRITUAL GUIDANCE AND
INSTRUCTION, MY MIND LEARNED TO DWELL
UPON RELIGIOUS THEMES WITH PLEASURE, WHILE
MY HEART FOUND PEACE IN BELIEVING.
THIS VOLUME IS INSCRIBED, AS A TRIBUTE OF
GRATEFUL AFFECTION, BY THE AUTHOR.

4

"We have been taught, consciously or unconsciously, intentionally or unintentionally, to seek rather what virtue gives than what virtue is; the reward rather than the service, the felicity rather than the life, the dowry, let me say, rather than the bride."

—T.T. STONE.

"His practice was of a more divine extraction, drawn from the word of God, and wrought up by the assistance of his Spirit; therefore, in the head of all his virtues I shall set that which was the head and spring of them all, his Christianity; for this alone is the true royal blood that runs through the whole body of virtue, and every pretender to that glorious family, who has no tincture of it, is an impostor. This is that same fountain which baptizeth all the gentle virtues that so immortalize the names of the old philosophers; herein they are regenerated, and take a new name and nature. Dug up in the wilderness of nature, and dipped in this living spring, they are planted and flourish in the paradise of God. By Christianity I intend that universal habit of grace which is wrought in a soul by the regenerating Spirit of God, whereby the whole creature is resigned up into the divine will and love, and all its actions directed to the obedience and glory of its Maker."

—MEMOIRS OF COL. HUTCHINSON,
BY HIS WIDOW.

The weakness and helplessness of humanity, in relation to the fortunes of this life, have been a favorite theme with philosophers and teachers ever since the world began; and every term expressive of all that is uncertain, insubstantial, and unstable has been exhausted in describing the feebleness of man's power to retain in possession the good things of this life, or even life itself. However firmly the hand of man may seem to grasp power, reputation, or wealth; however numerous may be the band of children or friends that surrounds him, he has no certainty that he may not die friendless and a pauper. In fact, the most brilliant success in life seems sometimes to be permitted only that it may make the darkness of succeeding reverses the more profound.

Weak and helpless as we may be in the affairs of this life, there is, however, one thing over which we have entire control. Riches may take to themselves wings, though honest industry exert its best efforts to acquire and retain them; power is taken away from hands that seek to use it only for the good of those they govern; reputation may become tarnished, though virtue be without spot; health may vanish, though its laws, so far as we understand them, be strictly obeyed; but there is one thing left which misfortune cannot touch, which God is ever seeking to aid us in building up, and over which he permits us to hold absolute control; and this is Character. For this, and for this alone, we are entirely responsible. We may fail in all else, let our endeavors be earnest and patient as they may; but all other failures touch us only in our external lives. If we have used our best endeavors to attain success in the pursuit of temporal objects, we are not responsible though we fail. But if we do not succeed in attaining true health and wealth and power of Character, the responsibility is all our own; and the consequences of our failure are not bounded by the shores of time, but stretch onward through the limitless regions of eternity. If we strive for this, success is certain, for the Lord works with us to will and to do. If we do not strive, it were better for us that we had never been born.

Character is all we can take with us when we leave this world. Fortune, learning, reputation, power, must all be left behind us in the region of material things; but Character, the spiritual substance of our being, abides with us for ever. According as the possessions of this world have aided in building up Character,—forming it to the divine or to the infernal image,—they have been cursings or blessings to the soul.

Before we can understand how Character is to be built up, we must come to a distinct faith in its reality; we must learn to feel that it is more real than anything else that we possess; for surely that which is eternal is more real than that which is merely temporal; it may, indeed, be doubted whether that which is merely temporal has any just claim to be called real.

Many persons confound reputation with Character, and believe themselves to be striving for the reality of the one, when the fantasy of the other alone stimulates their desires. Reputation is the opinion entertained of us by our fellow- beings, while Character is that which we really are. When we labor to gain reputation, we are not even taking a first step toward the acquisition of Character, but only putting on coverings over that which is, and protecting it against improvement. As well may we strive to be virtuous by thinking of the reward of heaven, as to build up our Characters by thinking of the opinions of men. The cases are precisely parallel. In each we are thinking of the pay as something apart from the work, while, in fact, the only pay we can have inheres in the doing of the work. Virtue is its own reward, because its performance creates the kingdom of heaven within us, and we cannot attain to virtue until we strive after it for its own sake.

A wisely trained Character never stops to ask, What will society think of me if I do this thing, or if I leave it undone? The questions by which it tests the quality of an action are, whether it is just, and wise, and fitting, when judged by the eternal laws of right; and in accordance with this judgment will its manifestations ever be made. If the mind acquires the habit of deliberately asking and answering these questions in regard to common affairs, it acquires, by degrees, distinct opinions in relation to life, forming a regular system, in accordance with which the Character is shaped and built up; and unless this be done, the Character cannot become consistent and harmonious. It is never too late to begin to do this; but the earlier in life it is done, the more readily the character can be conformed to the standard of right which is thus established. Every year added to life ere this is attempted, is an added impediment to its performance; and until it is accomplished, there is no safety for the Character, for each year is adding additional force to careless or evil habits of thought and affection, and consequently of external life.

It is not going too far to say, that Character is the only permanent possession we can have. It is in fact our spiritual body. All other mental possessions are to the spiritual body only what clothing is to the natural body,—something put on and taken off as circumstances vary. Character changes from year to year as we cultivate or neglect it, and so does the natural body; but these changes of the body are something very different from the changes of our garments.

There is a transient and a permanent side to all our mental attributes. Take, for instance, manners, which are the most external of them all. So far as we habituate ourselves to courtesy and good-breeding because we shall stand better with the world if we are polite than if we are rude, we are cultivating a merely external habit, which we shall be likely to throw off as often as we think it safe to go without it, as we should an uncomfortably fitting dress; and our manners do not belong to our Characters any more than our coats belong to our persons. This is the transient side of manners. If, on the contrary, we are polite from an inward conviction that politeness is one of the forms of love to the neighbor, and because we believe that in being polite we are performing a duty that our neighbor has a right to claim from us, and because politeness is a trait that we love for its own inherent beauty, our manners belong to the substance of our Character,— they are not its garment, but its skin; and this is the permanent side of manners. Such manners will be ours in death, and afterwards, no less than in life.

In the same way, every personal accomplishment and every mental acquisition has its transient and its permanent side. So far as we cultivate them to enrich and to ennoble our natures, to enlarge and to elevate our understandings, to become wiser, better, and more useful to our fellow-beings, we are cultivating our Characters,—the spiritual essence of our being; but these very same acquisitions, when sought from motives wholly selfish and worldly, are not only as transient as the clothes we wear, but often as useless as the ornaments of a fashionable costume. The Character will be poor and famished and cold, however great the variety of such clothing or ornament we may put on. When the mind has learned to appreciate the difference between reputation and Character, between the Seeming and the being, it must next decide, if it would build up a worthy Character, what it desires this should be; for to build a Character requires a plan, no less than to build a house. A deep and broad foundation of sound opinions, believed in with the whole heart, can alone insure safety to the superstructure. Where such a foundation is not laid, the Character will possess no architectural unity,—will have no consistency. Its emotions will be swayed by the impulses of the moment, instead of being governed by principles of life. There is nothing reliable in such a Character, for it perpetually contradicts itself. Its powers, instead of acting together, like well-trained soldiers, will be ever jostling each other, like a disorderly mob.

The zeal for special reforms in morality that so strongly characterizes the present age, whatever may be its utility or its necessity, may not be without an evil effect upon the training of Character as a whole. The intense effort after reform in certain particular directions causes many to forget or to overlook altogether the fact that one virtue is not enough to make a moral being. It cannot be doubted that the present surpasses all former ages in its eagerness to put down several of the most prominent vices to which man is subject; but it may be well to pause and calmly examine whether a larger promise is not sometimes uttered by the zeal so actively at work in society, than will probably be made good by its results.

Nothing can be worthy the name of Reform that is not based on the Christian religion,—that does not acknowledge the laws of eternal truth and justice,—that does not find its life in Christian charity, and its light in Christian truth. The tendency of reform at the present day is too often to separate itself from religion; for religion cannot work fast enough to satisfy its haste; cannot, at the end of each year, count the steps it has advanced in arithmetical numbers. The reformer asks not always for general growth and advancement in Christian Character; but demands special evidences, startling results, tangible proofs. These things all have their value, and the persons who strive for them doubtless have their reward; but if the kingdom of heaven and its righteousness were first sought, the good things so fiercely advocated and labored after by special reformers would be added unto them, as naturally as flowers and fruits, and the wealth of harvest, are added to the light and warmth of the advancing year.

Persons who devote themselves to one special branch of reform are apt to lose the power of appreciating any virtue save that one which they have selected as their own, and which they seem to love, not so much because it is *a* virtue as because it is *their* virtue. They soon lose all moral perspective, and resemble him who holds some one object so closely before his eyes that he can see nothing else, and cannot see that correctly, while he insists that nothing else exists worthy of being seen.

There is ever an effort going on in the mind of man to find some substitute for that universal obedience to the laws of faith and charity which the Scriptures demand; and this temptation adapts itself specially to every different class of believers. Thus the Jew, if the higher requisitions of the Law oppress him, thinks to secure himself from its penalties by the exactness of his ritual observances. The unfaithful Romanist hopes to atone for a life of sin by devoting his property to the Church, or to charity, when he dies. The Lutheran and the Calvinist, when false to the call of duty, think to be forgiven their neglect of the laws of charity by reason of the liveliness of their faith. So the modern reformer sometimes seems to suppose himself at liberty to neglect the cure of any of the vices that he loves, because he fancies that he may take the kingdom of heaven by violence through his devotion to the destruction of some special vice which he abhors. Thus temperance is at times preached by men so intemperate in their zeal, that they are unwilling to make public addresses on the Sabbath, because on that day they are trammelled by the constraint of decency, which prevents them from entering freely into the gross and disgusting details in which they delight. We have the emancipation of negroes sometimes preached by men fast bound in fetters of malignity and spiritual pride. We have the destruction of the ruling influence of the clergy inculcated by men dogmatic as Spanish Inquisitors. We are taught that the doctrine of the inspiration of the Scriptures is a mere figment, by those who are firmly convinced that their own inspiration is perfect and unfailing. The result of all this is the development of characters as deformed as are the bodies of victims to hydrocephalus or goitre; while, in painful contrast to such victims, these morally distorted patients bear about their deformities in the most conspicuous manner, as if they were rare beauties. So pagan nations, when they embody their ideas of superhuman attributes, often construct figures having several heads or hands, or enormously enlarge some particular member of the frame, fancying that they thus express ideas of wisdom or power more perfectly than they could by forming a figure whose parts should all present a symmetrical development.

It is not that reformers over-estimate the evil of any of the vices against which they contend; for in the abstract that is impossible; but that they under-estimate the evil of all other vices in relation to that one against which they arm themselves. The tree of evil has many branches, and the trimming away one of them may only make the rest grow more vigorously. There can be no thorough progress in reform until the evil of the whole tree is perceived and acknowledged, and the whole strength is turned to digging it up by the roots.

If a man devote himself actively to the reform of some special vice, while he at the same time shows himself indifferent to other vices in himself or in his neighbors, it is evident that his virtue is only one of seeming. We are told that he who is guilty of breaking one commandment is guilty of all; because if we disregard any one commandment of the Lord habitually, persisting in the preference of our own will to his, it is evident we have no true reverence for him, or that we act in conformity to his commandments in other points only because in them our will happens not to run counter to his; and this is no obedience at all.

If we find men leaving no stone unturned in promoting the cause of temperance, who do not hesitate to cheat and slander their neighbors, temperance is no virtue in them; but is the result of love of wealth, or of property, or of reputation, or of the having no desire for strong drink; because if a man abstain from intemperance from love to God, he will abstain from cheating and slandering from love to the neighbor. "He that loveth not his brother whom he hath seen, how can he love God whom he hath not seen?"

So, too, slavery is an enormous evil, and it is very easy for one who dwells in the free States to cover with opprobrium those who hold slaves; but if the abolitionist indulges in a violence of invective that compels one to fear that his heart is burning with hatred towards his Southern brothers, he stands quite as low in the moral scale as a *cruel* slaveholder, and possibly lower than a *kind* one.

The intemperate, and often malignant, violence with which men preach, and lead on crusades, against special vices, proves them ignorant of, or indifferent to, the significance of virtue as a whole. It does not enter into their hearts to conceive of the beauty of that growth in grace which results in the complete stature of a man,—that is, of an angel. In their haste to produce great growth in some particular direction, they overlook the fact, that in precise proportion to such growth must be the dwarfing of the other members of the soul. Man was created in the image and likeness of God; and he becomes truly a man only so far as, through the grace of God, his whole being voluntarily assumes that resemblance to the All-perfect for which he was designed. So long as he makes no effort to become regenerate, after he has arrived at an age to be at liberty to choose between good and evil, he turns himself more and more away from God, and becomes less and less like him. While in this state, he may possess many seeming virtues, may enjoy an untarnished reputation, may win the love of many friends; but is none the less the hollow image of that which should be the substance of a man. He is following only the devices of his own heart,—seeking only the good things of this world; and there is no virtue in anything that he does, though he may seem to devote all that he has, or all that he is, to purposes of charity or reform. Man begins to be truly virtuous,—to be truly a man, only when, relying on the strength of the Lord to sustain his endeavors, he begins to avoid sin because it is abhorrent to God, and to fulfil the commandments because they are the words of God. Then only he begins to form himself into the symmetrical figure of a man; and to become perfect after the manner in which the Heavenly Father is perfect.

The virtues all lock into each other. They cannot stand alone. Like the stones of an arch, no one of them can be wanting without making all the rest insecure. That Character alone is trustworthy in which each virtue takes its relative position, and all are held in place and confirmed by the key-stone of a living faith in the great central fact, that there is a God of infinite goodness and truth, whose commandments are the laws of life in this world and the world to come.

We cannot religiously obey one commandment unless we desire to obey all, because in order to obey one religiously we must obey it from reverence to the divine authority whence it emanates; and when such reverence is aroused in the heart, it sends the currents of spiritual life to every member of the spiritual frame, permeating the whole being, and suffering no disease to remain upon the soul. He, therefore, who devotes himself to some one object of reform enters upon an undertaking involving one of the most subtle temptations by which man is ever assailed. Spiritual pride will lie in wait for him every moment, telling him how clean he is compared with those against whose vices he is contending; and unless he is very strong in Christian humility, he will soon learn this oft-repeated lesson, and will go about the world with the spirit of the Pharisee's prayer ever in his heart,— "God, I thank thee that I am not as other men, intemperate, a slaveholder, a contemner of the rights of the weak. I am not, like many men, contented with fulfilling the common, every-day duties of life. They are too small for me. I seek to do great things; and to show my devotion to thee by going armed with all the power the law allows, to put down vice by force, and drive it from the face of the earth."

There is a class of men who assume to be, and are received by many as, philanthropists, who appear to delight in detecting and publishing to the world the vices of their fellow-beings. They seem to love to hate; and to find, in vilifying the reputations of those to whom they are opposed, a pleasure that can be compared to nothing human; but rather to the joy of a vulture as he gloats over, and rends in pieces, his carrion prey. While reading or listening to the raging denunciations of such persons, one is painfully reminded of the spirit that a few generations ago armed itself with the fagot and the axe in order to destroy those who held opinions in opposition to the dominant power. The axe and the fagot have disappeared; but, alas for human nature! the spirit that delighted in their use has hot wholly passed away; the flame and sword it uses now are those of malignity and hatred; it does not scorch or wound the body, but only burns and slays the reputations of those whom it assails. Forgetting that the Lord has declared, "judgment is mine," it hesitates but little to pass its condemnations upon those who differ from itself; and if Christian commandments are urged against it, it passes them by with a sneer, or openly sets them aside as too narrow and imperfect for the present age. While shrinking from the dangers that lie in wait for those who devote themselves to one idea in morality or reform, we should beware of falling into the opposite extreme of indifference on these same points; and should be sure to give them their full share of consideration. The ultra conservatism, that holds fast to existing customs and organizations merely because they are old, or from the love of conservation, is quite as fatuous as the radicalism that would destroy the old merely because it is old, or from the love of destruction. He whose conscience knows no higher sanction or restraint than the Statute Book, is not enough of a Christian to be a good citizen; while he who does not respect the Statute Book as the palladium of his country, is not a citizen worthy the name of Christian. While striving to remain unbiased by the clamor of party, or the violence of individuals, we should with equal care avoid the opposite error of looking with approval, or even with indifference, upon usages or institutions whose only claim to our forbearance lies in laws or popular opinions whose deformity should be discovered, and whose power should melt away beneath the light and warmth of a Christian sun.

True religious life consists in doing the will of God every moment of our lives. His will must bear upon us everywhere and at all times. Where the mind is absorbed in some one object of reform, this constant devotion to duty is almost, if not quite, impossible. The mind becomes so warped in one direction that it loses the habit, and almost loses the power, of turning in any other. Hence we rarely hear the word *duty* from the lips of the reformer. He constantly descants upon rights or wrongs, while duties seem forgotten. Thus we hear perpetually of the rights or of the wrongs of man or of woman, of the citizen, or of the criminal, and of the slave; but the duties of these classes seem to have passed out of sight. Now it is only when all shall fulfil their several duties that the rights of all can be respected; and if peace on earth, and good-will towards men are ever to reign, it must be when piety and charity shall go hand in hand,—when the human race shall unite as one to fulfil its duties towards God and towards each other.

Violence of every kind springs from a desire to do one's own will. Egotism is the sure accompaniment of wrath. The love of God never constrained any man to villify his brother. He who is bent on the performance of duty,—who desires simply to do the will of God, is firm as a rock, but never violent. He prays, with the poet,—

"Let not this weak, unknowing hand,
Presume thy bolts to throw;
And deal damnation round the land,
On each I judge thy foe."

He remembers that judgment belongs to God; and that the Lord taught us to pray, "Forgive our trespasses as we forgive those who trespass against us"; and surely none can hurl denunciation upon a fellow-sinner if from his heart he offers that prayer.

Possibly the ground may be taken that we should forgive our own personal enemies, but not the enemies of the Lord, against whom the reformer directs his wrath. But is the arm of the Lord shortened that he cannot avenge his own wrongs? and who among mortals is so pure or so strong that he may dare to say, the Lord has need of him for a champion?

It is deemed just that a soldier should suffer severe punishment if he act without orders, taking upon himself the authority of a commanding officer. How much more is he worthy of condemnation who puts himself in place of God, and under pretence of doing him service, presumes to transgress his explicit commands.

We are prone to fancy that when we are fond of talking about any object we are fond of the object itself; but this by no means follows of course. We may delight in talking about philanthropy while our hearts are burning with hatred, or about temperance while intoxicated with passion, or about abolitionism while we have no respect for the liberty of those around us, and no comprehension of that liberty wherewith Christ makes his children free; and all this because we are working from the blind impulses of an unregenerate spirit. When the spirit becomes regenerate,—taught of God,—it perceives the unity of virtue, and can never again regard it as a dismembered fragment. Then it knows, that to do wrong that good may come of it is striving to cast out Satan by Beelzebub,—an effort that must surely fail. Then it feels that evil is really overcome only by good. How different will be the reformatory zeal of this state of the spirit from that which preceded it. Formerly, no sooner was the subject of reform mentioned than the neck stiffened and the head tossed itself backward with the excitement of pride and combativeness, while the tongue poured forth whatever phrases anger might suggest. Now, how different is the attitude and expression, as with words of gentleness and love it strives to draw others to perceive the beauty of purity and justice. Formerly, the whole effort of the mind was to compel others to come into agreement with itself; now, it strives to win them into harmony with God. Once, it believed that indignation could be righteous; now, it knows that anger and heavenly mindedness dwell far apart; and, if they approach each other, one must perish.

If we would train character into genuine goodness, we should observe whether evil in ourselves or others offends us because it is contrary to our own ideas, or because it is opposed to the will of God. If the former be the case, we shall find ourselves angry; if the latter, we shall be sorrowful. No one can be angry from love to God. Anger is in its very nature egotistic and selfish, and has in it nothing of holiness. Penitence for sin is ever meek and humble, and so is regret for the sins of others. The moment we find ourselves angry, either for our own sins or for the sins of others, we may be sure there is something wrong in our state, and we should stop at once to analyze our feelings, and find where the trouble lies. If we do this conscienciously, we shall be sure to find some selfish or worldly passion at the root of the matter. We shall find that something else than love to God excited our indignation.

If we find ourselves indulging, habitually and with satisfaction in any one sin, we may be sure that we have not true hatred for any sin; for sin is hateful because it is contrary to the infinite wisdom and goodness of God. If we abhor it for this reason, we shall abhor all sin; and if we find ourselves hating some sins and loving others, we may be sure that we hate those which are repugnant to our own tastes, and love those which are in conformity with them. Thus our measure of sin is in ourselves, and not in God; and we are putting ourselves in place of God,—worshipping the idol self, instead of our Father in heaven.

The Lord was very explicit in his teachings regarding the necessity of the denial of self; but this is the last thing in which we are willing to obey him. We profess to be willing and eager to do a great deal of good; but when conscience tells us that we must do the will of God every moment of our lives, we turn away with a sorrowful countenance; for there are many things in which we wish to follow our own wills without stopping to consult the will of God, and we wish to believe that we can do this and yet be quite virtuous enough to insure salvation. While the natural man is strong within us, we are ever striving to serve God and mammon; but when the spiritual man is born, we are willing to give up all else and follow the Lord. Then, we feel that we cannot be truly virtuous, because we are, in some points, very scrupulous, while in others we are very indifferent; for we perceive that goodness is the harmonious development of the whole Character into accordance with the will of God.

So long as we labor for ourselves we shall be, at best, only special reformers, and cultivators of special virtues; but when we are ready to deny ourselves, and to do the will of God, all sin will become abhorrent to us, and we shall grow in grace daily until we become perfected in that symmetrical form of man, which is the image and likeness of God; and every faculty of the heart and of the head will then be baptized into the name of the Father, of the Son, and of the Holy Spirit.

THE HUMAN TRINITY.

"It is this trinity of man,—for man is the image of his God, in whom is the essential Trinity,—under which his whole character must be studied."

—KINMONT.

Man being created in the image and likeness of God, we must of necessity find in him a finite organization corresponding with the infinite organization of the Creator. In the Infinite Divine Trinity there are the Divine Goodness or Love, the Divine Truth or Wisdom, and the Divine Operation or the manifestation of the other two in and upon the universe: in other words, the Father, Son, and Holy Spirit. In the human, finite trinity, we have, corresponding with these, Affection, Understanding, and Use, or external life. Divinity being the embodiment of infinite order, its parts act in a sequence of absolute perfection; that is, absolute love by means of absolute wisdom exhibits itself in absolute use. Speaking with exactness, the word sequence is out of place in this connection, because with the Divinity, love, wisdom, and operation are simultaneous; but he has separated them in his ultimate manifestations, and we are obliged to separate them in our analysis, in order that they may in any degree come within the compass of human comprehension.

Man, in his primeval innocence, was a genuine image and likeness of the All-perfect Divinity; perfect after the same manner, but on a lower plane. There was then no antagonism between the creature and the Creator; and the finite naturally and joyfully obeyed the infinite; for in obedience to the will of the Heavenly Father it found sustenance for the soul as manifestly as in meat and drink for the body. The progress of time saw the creature turn from the love of God to the love of self,—from seeking the truth of God to seeking out its own vain imaginations, and from performing the orderly uses of a life of charity to all the disorderly indulgencies of selfish passion. Instead of worshipping the living God, man now invented idols representing his own evil passions, and bowed before them in adoring admiration; for the attributes wherewith he clothed them were fitting forces to stimulate his progress along the pathway he had chosen, where life was made hideous by the lowering shadows of rapine and murder.

The first Church, represented by Adam and Eve, is the general type of every Church that has followed it, and of every unregenerate individual in those Churches. Instead of looking to God as the source of all wisdom, there is ever the desire to eat of, or make our own, the fruit of the tree of knowledge, that we may know of *ourselves* good from evil; and that we may do of ourselves what seems to us right; and instead of penitence for sin and an endeavor after reformation, there is a striving to conceal our unfaithfulness. The covering assumed by those who, in Scripture, stand as the parents of mankind, is the perpetual type of the subterfuges we all invent to hide our disobedience from our God, from our neighbors, nay, even from ourselves. The primal image and likeness of God has become so defaced, distorted, and broken, that it is often hard to find a remnant still testifying to its Divine origin. Let us rise up from among these shattered fragments, and contemplate for a while the means of bringing the poor, fallen human nature into harmony with the divine;—let us develop, if we can, a system that may aid us in training our faculties, so that the Affections shall be pure, the Understanding wise, and Life the harmonious exponent of both.

In the attempt to restore our being to its original symmetry, the intellectual part of the nature must not be cultivated at the expense of the affectional, nor should the affectional be suffered to run riot with the intellectual. Love must be wise, and wisdom must be affectionate, or life will fail of its end. External morality has no reliable foundation unless it be built on morality of thought and affection. Apart from these, it is either the result of a happy organization that demands no disorderly indulgence, or it is the figleaf garment of deceit, put on by those who strive to seem rather than to be.

In the just training of Character, if we first learn to understand the capacities and relations of Affection, Thought, and Life, and look within our own natures until we learn to comprehend how everything pertaining to our being belongs to one of these departments, we shall better appreciate the difficulties to be overcome before we shall be willing to make everything that we do the honest outbirth of everything that we are. Pretence and hypocrisy, subterfuge and falsehood, will then disappear, and life will become the adequate expression of symmetrical Character.

The intellectual part of our being may be better understood if divided into two departments, viz., Thought and Imagination,—the subjective and the objective. Thought can be lifted up into the Affections, and made manifest in Life only through the medium of the Imagination. Thought is at first a pure abstraction, a subjective idea,—something entirely within the mind, and having no relation to conduct,—a seed sown, but not germinated; and while it remains thus it has no influence upon the Affections. If, however, it germinate, the next step in its existence is to become an objective idea; and now it has lost its abstract quality and become an image. In its first state it is neither agreeable nor disagreeable to the mind, but so soon as it takes a distinctive form it becomes either pleasing or displeasing, and is either cast away and forgotten, or retained arid expanded by the Affections, whose office it is to cause Thought to become a vital reality, ready to show itself in the external life so soon as a fitting occasion calls for its manifestation.

Thought is like water. Sometimes it glides over the mind as over a bed of rock; neither softening nor fertilizing; but when it is made a possible reality by the Imagination, and a vital reality by the Affections, it is now like a stream, flowing through rich farms and gardens, fertilizing wherever it comes; and again, like waterfalls, furnishing power to set ideas in motion, that shall give nutriment and warmth to the souls of millions.

The Lord, when he would condense religion into its narrowest compass, commands us to love the Heavenly Father with the whole heart and soul and mind and strength. Can this signify anything else than that Affection, Imagination, and Thought, in their whole strength, or brought down into the ultimates of life, must be consecrated to the Divine Creator of them all? So St. Paul, when he would sum up the whole Christian system in a single phrase, exclaims: "Faith, Hope, Charity. The greatest of these is Charity." Faith here expresses the religion of Thought, Hope the religion of the Imagination, and Charity the religion of the Affections, which is greatest of all because it is the vitalization of the other two.

Every act that we voluntarily perform, whether good or evil, first entered the mind as an abstract Thought; it was then shaped by the Imagination until it became a definite idea; next, it was claimed as a child by the Affections; and lastly, it was by the Affections made to come out into a use of love or an abuse of hate.

Many thoughts die in the mind without passing through all these stages. We sometimes hear a sermon that fills our Thoughts as we listen, and yet we forget it all as we turn away from the church door; for it went no deeper than our Thoughts. At another time, what we hear goes with us to our homes, haunts us through the week, and perhaps is made a standard whereby to measure the virtues or the vices of our neighbors; possibly even, we try ourselves by its rule, and our consciences are roused to pierce us with the sharp pang of remorse. All this, however, brings no change over our lives. Here Thought has passed into Imagination, has become a reality to the mind; but as yet the Affections do not warm towards it, and so it dies in the second stage of existence. Yet, again, we listen to the voice of the preacher, and his words abide in the soul until they quicken our Affections, and as we muse the fire burns. Then are our eyes lightened to perceive how all that we have heard may become realized in life; and warmed by the heavenly flame that has descended upon our altar, our souls kindle with charity, and we go forth to realize the hope that is within us in works of angelic use.

This process of the mind is not confined to the religious part of our being. It goes on perpetually in our intellectual no less than our moral nature. Our success in using whatever we learn in every department, the wisdom or the folly of everything we do, whether relating to intellectual, to religious, or to practical life, depends on the faithfulness with which we apply these three powers to whatever is presented to them.

Look in upon the assembled members of a school, of any grade from primary to collegiate, and you will see one set of pupils with stolid faces conning their tasks, as if they were indeed tasks in the hardest sense of the term, and then reciting them word for word, in a monotonous tone, as if their voices came from automata, and not from living throats. These are they who study only with their Thoughts, and whose Imaginations and Affections are untouched by all that passes through their minds. Scattered among the preceding another class may be found, with quickly glancing eyes, who seem all alive to everything they study, who recite with earnest tones, and whose faces are bright with expression. Here the Imagination is at work, and everything the mind seizes upon stands there at once a living picture. These are the brilliant scholars, who carry off all the prizes, and win all admiration. There is still a third class, of a calmer aspect. Its members may not shine so brightly, but there is more warmth in their rays. They will not learn so much nor so rapidly as those of the second class, but their whole being is permeated by what they know. They are constantly studying the relations of the things that they learn to each other and to life; and are endeavoring to form themselves in accordance with the rationality they thus acquire; for their Affections have fastened themselves upon it, and it is therefore becoming a part of their being.

When these three classes of pupils become men and women, and go forth into the various walks of life, the first, if they attempt any handicraft, are the botchers and bunglers, who bring little more than their hands to anything that they do; and who, therefore, do nothing well. They are the dead weights of society, that must be helped through life by their more active

24

neighbors. If they are scholars, they are collectors of facts, which they pile up in their memories as a miser heaps his gold, for no end but the pleasure of heaping. They make physicians without resource, lawyers without discernment, preachers who dole out divinity in its baldest and heaviest forms.

Those of the second class are always better in theory than in practice; for with them zeal ever runs before knowledge. They will delight in telling how a thing should be done, but will find it very difficult to do it themselves. A blacksmith of this class will tell with great exactness how a horse should be shod, but if trusted to perform that office, ten to one the poor animal will go limping from his hands. So a carpenter of the same class will be full of plans and fancies that he will wish to carry out for the benefit of his employers; but his work, when completed, though perhaps elegant and ornamental, will probably be inappropriate in appearance, and not adapted to the use for which it was intended. From this class come inventors of machines that are never heard of after they get into the patent-office, schemers and speculators whose plans end in ruin, boon companions, brilliant talkers, sparkling orators, elegant and ornate poets who sing blithely for their own day and generation, preachers and statesmen who are ever led away by Utopian and millennial dreams; in short, men who may shine while they live, but are seldom remembered when they die.

The third class are men of mark in whatever walk of life they are found; —men to be relied upon for whatever they may undertake. They are men who can produce in Life what their Understandings know and imagine; or, rather, who know how to select from their stores of Thought and Imagination whatever may be realized in Life. If they are mechanics, their work is the best of its kind, and precisely adapted to the use for which it was intended; if they are machinists, their inventions are those that ameliorate the condition of society; if merchants or speculators, they do not run after bubbles; if devoted to intellectual pursuits, they are divines whose thoughts thrill the souls of men for centuries, founders of new schools of philosophy, lawgivers, and

25

statesmen who are remembered with gratitude as the fathers of nations, poets whose words are destined to live so long as the language in which they write is spoken,—nay, who shall cause their language to be studied ages after all who spoke it have passed from the face of the earth.

The women who belong to these several classes are characterized in like manner, though their more retired lives prevent them from displaying their traits so conspicuously. Those of the first class are dress-makers whose work never fits, milliners whose bonnets look as if they were not intended for the wearers, servants who do nothing rightly unless the eye of their mistress is upon them, teachers whose pupils are taught as if they were beings without life or reason; and in their highest relations, as wives and mothers, they are those with whom nothing goes as it should, whose daily lives are but a succession of mistakes and catastrophies, whose husbands never find a comfortable home to which they may return for repose after a day of toil, whose children are "dragged up, not brought up."

In the second class are servants who have a quick perception of what is to be done, and who make all that is directly apparent to the eye look well, but a closer observation shows many an unswept corner and neglected duty; dress-makers and milliners whose work is ornamental, tasteful, and becoming, though the ornamentation is apt to be too great for the value of the material, and the work will now and then come in pieces for lack of being thoroughly finished; teachers who infuse brightness and quickness into their scholars, but whose instructions are more showy than solid. In their housekeeping they understand "putting the best foot foremost," and making a great deal of ornament where there may be but little of anything else; but they lack the practical skill that makes a housekeeper successful in the essentials that constitute comfort. They will seek to make their children accomplished ladies and gentlemen, who will be agreeable in society, rather than well-trained men and women, capable of meeting the duties and emergencies of life.

The third class of women are the reliable ones, wherever they may be found. They do everything they attempt well, because there is a sense of fitness and propriety in them which is disturbed by things badly done, and which gives them an almost intuitive faith, that if a thing is worth doing at all, it is worth doing well. They are not eye-servants, but faithful in all things. Thoroughness pervades whatever they do, in all departments of life. They are not satisfied with making a dress or a bonnet that is becoming, unless it is well finished and appropriate. They are the thorough teachers who are willing to have their schools examined every day in the year, who seek to know the capacities of their pupils, and to educate them accordingly. They are the mothers whose children are obedient and trained for the uses of life no less than for its pleasures; the wives whose husbands are happy in their homes if they are capable of being happy anywhere.

When we contemplate these three classes of human beings, we perceive that only one of them can be said to lead successful lives. Two classes, and both of them painfully numerous, fail. The question rises to the mind with fearful solemnity, were they created for this end,—created to fail? Can we for a single moment believe that a Father of infinite justice and mercy ever created one individual among his children, an accountable being, neither insane nor idiotic, and yet so imperfect that he *must* fail? Surely it were blasphemy to hold such an act possible. Infinitely various are the works of his hand in the forms of humanity, as in every other department of the universe, but even so manifold are the varieties and degrees of service which he prepares for every one to do. There is a place and a use for every one, and whoever fails of finding a place and a use fails, not because he was created incompetent, but because he refuses to cultivate the powers wherewith he is endowed. Indolence and selfishness, the moth and rust of Character, are corroding and devouring the delicate organization of the internal man, which can retain the wholeness and brightness of its powers only by constant use. We are weak and useless, not because we were created to be so, but because we do not listen to the voice of conscience when it tells us to serve

27

the Lord with *all* our strength, in the very place where we now are, and at the very time that now is. It is not because the power of growth is not in them that our talents do not multiply, but because we fold them in a napkin of indifference, and bury them in the earth of our lower nature. Understanding and Affection are within us all, and if they do not develop into a life of use, into a Character that will fit us for heaven,—and this is what we should always keep before our minds as the only genuine success,—it is because we have not striven as we might and ought.

Understanding and Affection are within us all, differing, not in kind, but only in degree; and they are constantly at work, involuntarily if we do not voluntarily assume their control. In the little child they work as involuntarily as the heart beats and the lungs respire; but so soon as the child is old enough to begin to know the difference between right and wrong, the action of these powers should begin to be voluntary; should begin to be under the guidance of conscience.

Some persons call these powers into voluntary action from motives of mere worldly wisdom. Every one does so who places some object before himself, and cultivates his powers with a special view to attain perfection therein. The pickpocket, the gambler, the housebreaker, must do it before they can attain skill in their depravity. The worldling does it who follows an honorable profession with all his heart and soul and mind and strength, seeking only such rewards as Mammon bestows upon his votaries. Whether all these are to be successful in attaining the rewards they seek, is a matter of entire uncertainty; for Providence permits or withholds worldly success in a way that we cannot anticipate, nor but imperfectly understand. We may bear the heavy yoke of Mammon until it wear into the very marrow of our bones, and yet gain nothing but poverty and disgrace. They, however, who by a voluntary action of the powers endeavor to become perfected in the stature of Christian men and women,— who seek first the kingdom of heaven and its righteousness, using all things of this world only as rounds of that ladder whose summit is in the heavens, even while its base rests upon the earth, are sure of the reward they seek; and the yoke that they bear will grow more light and easy with each revolving year.

There are many persons who seem to belong by turns to each of the three great classes that have been described. These exercise their powers involuntarily. They cannot be depended upon, for they are not balanced Characters. If they happen to like what they are doing, or happen to feel in the mood of doing it, they will do it well; otherwise, they do not care how badly their work is performed, if it only can be got through with. They have not waked to the consciousness that we have no right to do anything badly, because whenever we do so we impair our own faculties, and thereby diminish our powers of usefulness; while, if the act concerns any one beside ourselves,—as almost all acts do,—we are wronging our neighbor.

Many persons are so fortunate, women especially almost always so, as to have enough employment placed before them by the circumstances of their position, without any effort of choice on their part, to occupy their time, and to train their faculties. Those who are not thus set to work by circumstance should be governed in the selection of their employment by their own inclination and talents. What we love to do we can learn to do well, and our work will then be agreeable to us. Many persons are governed in the choice of employment for themselves or for their children by a stronger consideration for what is honorable in the eyes of the world than by talent or taste. Thence it often results that persons fail ever to fulfil the duties they have chosen in a way to be satisfactory to any one beside themselves, perhaps not even to themselves. If they have sufficient force of Character to do well in spite of not doing what they like, they are still never so happy as they would have been had inclination been consulted. Where the heart is really in the employment, work is not a burden, but a natural and pleasant exercise of the powers; and it becomes comparatively easy to serve the Lord with all the strength.

Those who are not constrained to work, should remember that a life of idleness cannot be a life of innocence; for the idle cannot serve the Lord. A life that does not cultivate one's own

29

capacities, and aid either in supplying the wants or cultivating the capacities of some one beside self, is no preparation for heaven; for the heavenly life is one of perpetual advance, because of untiring use.

There is no station in life where there is not a constant demand for the exercise of charity. We cannot be in company an hour with any person without some such demand presenting itself to us. The daily intercourse of life places it constantly in our power to make some person more or less happy than he now is, and accordingly as we may choose between these two modes of action we are fulfilling or setting aside the law of charity.

No class of human beings bears a more heavy weight of responsibility than that which is placed beyond the necessity of effort; and there is none whose position has a stronger tendency to blind it to the calls of duty. Although every gift bestowed upon us by providence, whether of mind, body, or estate, is but another talent, for the employment of which we must be one day called to account, yet these added talents too often excite in us a feeling of superiority which induces us to demand that others should minister to us, and causes us to forget that he who would be greatest must be so by doing more and greater services than others, and not by receiving them.

Persons whose position places them beyond the need of effort, would do well to select some special study or employment to occupy and develop their mental life, and save them from the inanity, ennui, and selfishness that are sure to follow in the footsteps of idleness. Poverty of mind is rendered all the more prominent and disgusting if accompanied by external wealth; and to such a mind wealth is but a means to folly, if to nothing worse.

Neither wealth nor poverty, neither strength nor weakness, neither genius nor the want of it, neither ten talents nor one, can excuse any human being from training his faculties in a way to develop them to the utmost, and forming them into a symmetrical whole, the type of a true humanity.

In the following essays it may seem to the reader that there is contradiction in treating each power of the mind as though its perfect training resulted in the upbuilding of a perfect Character; but the union between these capacities is so intimate that one cannot be rightly trained unless all the others are trained at the same time. We cannot think wisely unless we imagine truly, and love rightly, as well as warmly. We cannot love rightly unless we think justly, and imagine purely; nor can we imagine purely unless we love that which is pure. We cannot do all this unless we live out what we think, imagine, and love; for the inner life always acts narrowly and superficially unless it be widened and deepened by an efficient external life. What we do must follow closely in the footsteps of what we know, if we would arrive at breadth and depth of knowledge. So fast as we put in practice what we know we shall be able to receive more knowledge. We are told by the Lord that our knowledge of truth shall be enlarged in proportion as we are obedient to the divine will. "If any man will do his will, he shall know of the doctrine."

The Divine attributes act simultaneously and equally always and everywhere, while the triune manifestation is a merciful adaptation of these attributes to the comprehension of fallen humanity. Were humanity truly regenerate, the action of its capacities would be simultaneous and homogeneous. Even in its present state these capacities are so interlaced that one cannot act strongly without inducing some action in the others; just as in the physical frame the brain, the heart, and the lungs can no one of them act unless all act in some degree; while in perfect health all act in the fulness of perfect harmony, no one organ rendering itself prominent by being more full of vitality and activity than another. Disease alone renders us conscious of the action of any one vital organ, and our moral diseases having destroyed the harmonious action of our moral powers, thereby rendering it impossible for us to appreciate the Divinity in the full harmony of unity, we have been mercifully permitted to attain to such knowledge as is possible to us through manifestations of the Divine attributes in trinity. In proportion as our faculties are trained to act in harmony we shall become unconscious of their separate functions; and in the same proportion we shall become capable of looking upon the Divinity in the

THOUGHT.

It is the grandeur of all truth which *can* occupy a very high place in human interests, that it is never absolutely novel to the meanest of minds: it exists eternally by way of germ or latent principle in the lowest as in the highest, needing to be developed, but never to be planted.

—DE QUINCEY.

Many persons seem to suppose that the power of Thought, or at least the power of thinking to any purpose, is a natural gift, possessed by few, and unattainable by the many. This idea is a very pernicious error, for one of the traits by which the human being is distinguished from the brute is the possession of this power; and the progress that every human being may make in learning to think well has no limit but the universal one of finite capacity.

The distinction made between thoughtful and thoughtless persons is commonly one of intellect alone; it should be quite as much one of morality. Considered intellectually, a thoughtless person cannot be successful in any but the very lowest walks of life. He brings nothing but his hands to what he does. If these be strong, he may dig, perhaps, as well as another man, but he can never make a good farmer; he may use the axe or the hammer to good purpose, but he can never become a master-workman. If he attempt anything more or higher than what his hands can do under the guidance of another's brain, his effort is sure to be followed by confusion and failure. Viewing a thoughtless person in a moral light, he cannot be religious, he cannot be virtuous, and, unless by accident, he cannot even be externally moral. He may, perhaps, perceive that the grosser forms of wickedness are to be avoided, but he can have no comprehension of the danger involved in the little vices of everyday life; and cannot understand how every one of these vices, small as it may seem, contains within itself the germ of some one of those great and shocking sins forbidden in the commandments. He will, therefore, without compunction, go on committing these small sins until the habit of evil becomes so fixed, that, if he does not end by committing great ones, it is more frequently from lack of temptation than from any worthier reason.

The thoughtless person can never be depended upon for anything. We never know where to find him, or what he will do in any particular position or relation of life. All we can anticipate of him is, that he will probably do something bad, or silly, or improper; accordingly as the act may bear upon morality, sense, or manners.

Before going further, let it be understood that a thoughtless person is not one without Thought. A human being without Thought is an impossibility. Most, if not all, idiots think. It is the lack of coherency, purpose, and effort in Thought that induces the habit of mind commonly known as thoughtlessness. Without Thought, Imagination, and Affection, one could not be a human being. Mankind differ from each other, not in kind, but in degree. It is the low degree of activity in either of these great divisions of the human mind that causes one to seem thoughtless, unimaginative, or without affection. The end of all training should be to develop each one of these faculties so that it shall coöperate with the others, and all as fully as possible. A just balance of power is the first requisite, and constant increase of it the second; just as in the physical frame we ask, first, for just proportion, and, as the product of this, for strength.

It is often said that no kind of sense is so rare as common sense; and this is true, simply because common sense is attainable by all far more, and is a natural gift far less, than most other traits of character. Common sense is the application of Thought to common things, and it is rare because most persons will not exercise Thought about common things. If some important affair occurs, people try then to think, but to very little purpose; because, not having exercised their powers on small things, their powers lack the development necessary for great ones. Hence, thoughtless people, when forced to act in an affair of importance, blunder through it with no more chance of doing as they should than one would have of hitting a small or distant mark at a shooting-match, if previous practice had not given the power of hitting objects that are large and near.

The thoughtless person perpetually acts and speaks as if it were of no consequence what is said or done. If any one venture to suggest a different mode of speech or action, the reply is pretty sure to be, "O, it is of no consequence!" As if an immortal being, to whom a few short years of probation had been given, the use or abuse of which must give character to an eternity to come, could do or say what would have no consequence! Let any one bring distinctly before himself the great truth that we stand ever in the presence of the Almighty, stewards of his bounty, children of his love, and could it be possible for him to believe that it is of no consequence how that love is returned, and how that bounty is used? Every word, every act of our lives, is either a use or an abuse of his bounty, a showing forth either of our love for or our indifference to him. Therefore, every word and act has a consequence, ending not with the hour or day, but stretching forward into eternity. Let this truth be admitted to the mind, and who could dare to be thoughtless. Who would not wish to return the infinite love poured out upon us, by consecrating all that we have and all that we are to the service of the Infinite Father? When this consecration takes place, all pure aspirations fill the heart, while the mind is ever thinking what is the best way in which the will of the Lord may be done. Thoughtlessness has no longer an abiding-place, for the mind now perceives that it must be about its Father's business, and Thought becomes a delightful and invigorating exercise, instead of the wearisome effort it seemed before.

If the mind hold to its integrity, without relapsing into its former state of blind indifference to its high vocation, the cultivation of the power of Thought will go on steadily and surely, and the mind will become constantly more and more clarified from all folly and silliness.

When a person brings everything habitually to the standard of right and wrong, he gradually learns to judge wisely of whatever subject he may hold under consideration, provided he does not seek for that standard in his own mind, but in the mind of the Lord, as he has given it to us in the Word of eternal life. When this standard is sought only in the human mind, nothing is fixed or permanent, and discord abounds in society much as it would if the length and breadth of the fingers of each individual were to be substituted for the standard inch and foot of the nation; but if the Bible be honestly and humbly received as the standard by which to judge of right and wrong, mankind would ever abide in brotherly love and harmonious union. The element of discord is not in God's work, but in the mind of man; and man becomes truly wise and capable of concord only so far as, forgetting the devices of his own understanding, he becomes a recipient of the truth that descends to him from on high.

It may be objected that the Bible has been the fruitful source of contention and war; and some may suppose it cannot therefore be a standard of union to the world; but it should be remembered that, when it has become a cause of dissension, it has been by the perversion of man, who has separated doctrine from life,—has put asunder that which God joined. No contention has ever risen in the world regarding religious life, but many and terrible ones regarding religious doctrine separated from life; and it is perfectly apparent, that, had those who were engaged in them, looked to religious life with the same earnestness they did toward doctrine, all these dissensions must have ceased. Christian life is, as it were, a building, of which faith is the foundation. The foundation is subservient to the superstructure, and should be strong and well laid; but has no value excepting as it is the support of a worthy building. The Lord is very explicit in all his teachings on the subject of life, and it is hardly possible that any one could faithfully study his words, and then exalt abstract doctrine into the place that belongs of right to Christian life.

Whoever studies the direct teachings of the Lord, recorded by the Evangelists, and makes them the rules of his Thoughts, must necessarily be wise. Everything connected with daily life, if his mind be really permeated with these teachings, takes its proper place before him. He sees what has a transient, and what a permanent value,—what is merely temporal, and what eternal; and so learns to appreciate the relative value of all things. Everything that occurs becomes a subject for his thoughts to work upon, and while working in heavenly light his mind grows in wisdom day by day. This action of Thought will not be confined to events as they occur around him, but whatever is read, all the events of the past, all art and science, are brought under the same analysis. The thoughtless person reads merely for the amusement of the moment, remembers little of what he reads, and that little to no purpose. A fact is, to such a man, a mere fact standing by itself, and having no relation to anything else. However much he may read, the thoughtless man can never be instructed. He is of those who, seeing, perceive not, and who, hearing, do not understand. The thoughtful person, on the contrary, reads everything with a purpose. His mind works upon what he reads, and he is instructed and made intelligent, even though he may see only with the light of this world. His intelligence will, however, be very different and very inferior in degree to that of the man who looks at objects in the light of heaven. He will measure things by an uncertain, varying standard, and will appreciate things only according to their temporal value. He will, therefore, never become truly wise. With those whose minds are nurtured by the words of the Lord, everything is judged by the standard of eternal truth. Whatever is learned is digested by the thoughts, and so the powers of the mind are strengthened and enlarged. Thus the mind becomes constantly more and more wise. The merely intellectual man has the desire to become wise, but his eye is not single, and therefore his mind is obscured by many clouds,—the dark exhalations of worldliness. When a man fixes his eye upon the Lord he is filled with light, and sees with a clearness of vision such as can be gained from no other source.

The cultivation of Thought lies at the root of all intellectuality, while it elevates and enlarges the sphere of the Affections. Affection is above Thought, but it is sustained and invigorated by its influence. Thought being the foundation upon which Affection is built, the strength, permanence and reliability of Affection must depend on the solidity and justice of the underlying Thought.

The mind may be stored with the most varied and extensive knowledge, and yet be neither improved nor adorned thereby. Robert Hall once remarked of an acquaintance, that he had piled such an amount of learning upon his brain, it could not move under the weight. It is little matter whether the amount of learning be large or small; the brain is only encumbered by it, unless it has taken it into its own texture, and made it by Thought a part of itself. Some persons love facts as a miser loves gold, merely because they are possessions; but without any desire to make use of them. A fact or thought is just as valuable in itself as a piece of money. Gold and silver are neither food, nor raiment, nor shelter; but we value them because through their means we can obtain all these. So facts and thoughts are neither rationality, nor wisdom, nor virtue, and their value lies in their being mediums whereby we may obtain them all.

Undigested learning is as useless and oppressive as undigested food; and as in the dyspeptic patient the appetite for food often grows with the inability to digest it, so in the unthinking patient an overweening desire to know often accompanies the inability to know to any purpose. Thought is to the brain what gastric juice is to the stomach,—a solvent to reduce whatever is received to a condition in which all that is wholesome and nutritive may be appropriated, and that alone. To learn merely for the sake of learning, is like eating merely for the taste of the food. The mind will wax fat and unwieldy, like the body of the gormand. The stomach is to the frame what memory is to the mind; and it is as unwise to cultivate the memory at the expense of the mind, as it would be to enlarge the capacity of the stomach by eating more food than the wants of the frame require, or food of a quality that it could not appropriate. To learn in order to become wise makes the mind active and powerful, like the body of one who is temperate and judicious in meat and drink. Learning is healthfully digested by the mind when it reflects upon what is learned, classifies and arranges facts and circumstances, considers the relations of one to another, and places what is taken into the mind at different times in relation to the same subjects under their appropriate heads, so that the various stores are not heterogeneously piled up, but laid away in order, and may be referred to with ease when wanted. If a person's daily employments are such as demand a constant exercise of the thoughts, all the leisure should not be devoted to reading, but a part reserved for reflecting upon and arranging in the mind what is read. The manner of reading is much more important than the quantity. To hurry through many books, retaining only a confused knowledge of their contents, is but a poor exercise of the brain; it is far better to read with care a few well-selected volumes.

There is a strong tendency towards superficial culture at the present day, which is the natural result of the immense amount of books and periodicals constantly pouring from the press, and tempting readers to dip a little into almost everything, and to study nothing. Much is said of the pernicious consequences arising from lectures and periodicals, as though a short account of anything must of necessity be a superficial one; but this is far from the truth. A quarto volume on one theme may be entirely superficial, while a lecture or review-article on the same theme may contain the whole gist of the matter. Prolixity is oftener superficial than brevity. Books are superficial if they relate only to the outside of a subject,—if they describe only its husk; and the reverse, if they give its kernel. Many an able review-article contains the kernel of a whole volume, and if the pleased reader of the review goes to the book itself, expecting to enjoy that in a degree proportionate to its size, he will often find he has got nothing but a dry husk for his pains.

Those who have little time for books, but who wish really to know many things, can accomplish a great deal by being careful to hunt for meats rather than for shells and husks; for though the outsides of things make a great show, and can be displayed by the pedant to great advantage before those who are superficial as himself, they contain no healthful nutriment for the mind. Take, for instance, the study of botany. Let a person master the whole vocabulary of the science, and know the arrangement of its classifications so well that he can turn at once to the description of any plant he may find. Let him do this until, like King Solomon, he knows every plant by name, from the "hyssop on the wall to the cedar of Lebanon"; but if at the same time he knows nothing more about them than the name, his knowledge of botany is entirely superficial, though he may have spent a vast deal of time and labor in its acquisition. Let another person have studied the physiology of plants till he has learned all that has yet been discovered of their curious and beautiful structure,—till he appreciates as far as mortals may the Divine wisdom, that even in the formation of a blade of grass transcends not only all that man with all his pride of science and mechanical skill can perform, but goes far—we cannot even guess how far—beyond all that human intellect can comprehend; and still more if the mind of this student be lifted upward in adoration as he learns, he is the true botanist, though he may have studied far less, if we count by time, than his superficial brother.

So it is with all the sciences. The kernel is what nourishes the mind,—the knowledge of what God has created, and not the mere power of repeating the classifications and vocabularies that man has invented to describe these creations: not that these also have not an eminent use; but still it is one that should always be esteemed secondary in all our studies.

So, too, it is with history. One may have all the important dates, names, and facts of the world's history at the tongue's end, and yet be none the wiser; for such knowledge is but the surface of history. To know history well, is to have so arranged its facts in the mind that it may be contemplated as a continuous exhibition of God's providence. It is to study the succession of events, not as separate units, but as links of one vast chain, on every one of which is inscribed a phrase discoursing of the progress of the human race, and showing the growth of man in the complex, from infancy to adolescence. Further than that, we can hardly venture to believe the race has yet advanced. Thus studied, history is the noblest of all sciences, since it treats of the highest of God's creations; but studied as a mere congeries of facts, all sciences are alike worthless; and from the mousings of the mere antiquarian to the dredgings of the student of the shelly coverings of the Mollusca, all end in naught.

When a person's employment is one that does not require a constant exercise of the thoughts, there is the greater need of a constant supply of nutritious food for the mind, that it may be growing all the time by reflection, and thus be saved from falling into a morbid state, such as too often results from long confinement to an occupation demanding little exertion of its powers. The farmer at his plough, the mechanic at his bench, the seamstress at her needle, and a host of others, too often suffer the thoughts to wander into realms of morbid egotism and discontent, when, if they would turn them upon moral or intellectual themes, they might be growing wiser and better every day.

It may be objected, that those who are obliged to work hard through the whole week cannot, on the Sabbath, take enough intellectual food to last them for Thought during the week. Every person can, if he will, find time for a chapter in the Bible every day, and therein lies wisdom, that all humanity combined can never exhaust, and which ever opens richer stores the more it is wrought upon. Then the human race are everywhere around us, and every individual is a volume to be read. We are vexed, and perhaps tormented, by the vices or foibles of those with whom we are thrown in contact. Let us not stop in vexation, but study our own hearts, and see if there is not some kindred vice or foible in ourselves that perhaps troubles our friends quite as much as this disturbs us; for it is often the case that our own vices, when we meet them in others, are precisely those which irritate us most; and we are almost always more irritable through our vices than through our virtues. Again, we find persons exciting our admiration through their virtues. Let us not stop in cold admiration, but reflect how we may engraft similar virtues upon our own souls. It is deep and earnest Thought alone that can teach us to know ourselves, and without this knowledge we are in constant danger of cherishing repulsive vices such as we should abhor in others, and of neglecting the culture of virtues such as in others we esteem indispensable. Society at large, too, is around us, and domestic circles, with all their complex relations, their jarring discords, or their heavenly harmonies; and all are full of food for Thought. The true and the false, the right and the wrong, are everywhere, and the highest wisdom is to be able to distinguish one from the other. He who has spent his whole life in intellectual pursuits may, in this greatest wisdom,—the only wisdom that belongs to eternity equally with time,—be the veriest fool; while he who has patiently and prayerfully and obediently studied no book but the Bible may be so taught of God that he shall possess all that man while on earth can possess of this highest wisdom.

It is beautifully said by William von Humboldt, that "exactly those joyful truths which are the most needful to man— the holiest and the greatest—lie open to the simplest, plainest mind; nay, are not unfrequently better, and even more entirely, grasped by such a one, than by him whose greater knowledge more dissipates his thoughts. These truths, too, have this peculiarity, that, although they want no profound research to attain to them, but rather make their own way in the mind, there is always something new to be found in them, because they are in themselves inexhaustible and endless."

While the Bible is left to us, while human beings surround us, while our own souls are to be cleansed, renewed, and saved, we miserably deceive ourselves if we think we lack material for Thought. We are thinking perpetually, whether we will or no, and let us look to it that we think to some good purpose. How much Thought is worse than wasted in planning how wealth, which too often profiteth not, may be acquired, while the true riches that the Lord is ever offering for our acceptance are forgotten! How often are the Thoughts poisoned with envying the lands of one's neighbor, while one's own soul is lying an uncultivated waste. How often is the mind cankered with vexation at the intellectual achievements of an old schoolmate, whom in school days we never deemed wiser than ourselves, when all that has wrought the present difference between us is, that he thought and strove while we dreamed and loitered.

In its purely religious action, Thought is the fountain of that Faith which forms the base of St. Paul's trinity of the primal elements of Character,—the foundation upon which hope and charity are to be elevated. How important, then, is it that this foundation should be wisely laid! Many persons think much in relation to religious subjects from the love of metaphysical reasoning; while their lives are not influenced by the doctrines they profess. This is an abuse of Thought, one of its fruits is bigotry. The more strongly a man confirms himself in any doctrine that he does not apply to life, the more elevated he becomes in his own estimation,—the more puffed up with spiritual pride,—the more full of contempt and hatred towards those who disagree with him. With such persons, purity of life is as nothing compared with faith in a certain set of dogmas. There are some who think much of the vices of life, but always in relation to their neighbors, and thereby engender that form of bigotry called misanthropy. Both these classes misuse the faculty of Thought, making it subserve the purposes of contempt and hatred and debasing narrow-mindedness, instead of ministering to Christian love, that hopeth all things of its brother, and judges as it would be judged.

The more we study human nature out of ourselves, and in the light of the Understanding, the less we love it; but the reverse takes place when we study our own hearts at the same time that we study the characters of our fellow-beings, and both in the light of Christian truth. We cannot hate our fellow-beings while we perceive that we are all of one family,—while we feel our own weakness and sinfulness; and we cannot despair of human nature while we believe that Infinite Wisdom has become its Redeemer and Saviour.

If Thought be strongly turned towards religious subjects, the mind must necessarily form to itself many doctrines which will be its true creed, whatever external form of Church creed it may avow, or even if it disavow all creeds. At the present day, it is not uncommon to hear creeds spoken of with contempt, as the effete remains of a past age; and the remark is often made, that it is of no consequence what a man believes if he do but lead a good life. The religious opinions we hold constitute the morality of our internal life; and it is difficult to understand how internal morality can be of no consequence, while external morality is of so much. It would seem that external morality is but a mask, unless it truly represent the internal morality. Still it is not surprising that many superficial observers should be found ready to express their aversion to creeds, when we consider the abuses into which Churches and Governments have rushed in their efforts to establish and maintain their favorite dogmas; or when we observe how the bigoted supporters of creeds become blinded to every other consideration, and learn to look upon life as of little importance when compared with doctrine. It was probably in contemplation of such bigotry that the Apostle exclaims, "Show me thy faith without works, and I will show thee my faith by my works." This saying is often quoted in defence of the idea that faith is of no consequence compared with works; but this is no logical deduction from the text. "I will show thee my faith by my works" expresses no disregard or undervaluing of faith, but asserts the great truth that faith becomes a living reality only when it forms itself into works. The quality of works depends, not on the works themselves, but upon the faith that inspires them. For instance, three men of equal wealth may each give the same sum of money to some charity. Externally the act is the same in each individual, yet the common sense of the very same persons who a few moments before may have asserted that faith is nothing, and works everything, does not hesitate to estimate it in a totally different manner. One of the donors has made up his mind that ease is the only good. He has taught himself to believe that it is wise to avoid all trouble, and to give rather than make the effort of resisting importunity; and he gives because he carries this belief into effect. Another is an ambitious man, who believes that power and the good opinion of society are the best among good things; and he gives to obtain the praise of men and the influence in society which follows praise. The third believes that the first good of life is making others happy, and with systematic benevolence examines every claim upon his bounty, and, if he finds it worthy, never dismisses it unsatisfied. It was the faith within the act that gave this distinctive quality to the three donations. The first put his faith in ease, the second in the opinion of the world, and the third in doing good to the neighbor; and the common sense of the community judges the actions accordingly. All the actions of life range themselves under one or other of the three heads represented by these gifts; namely, the love of self, or ease; the love of the world, or ambition; and the love of the neighbor, or true charity. Every man is probably governed in turn by each of these loves; but in every man one of them takes the lead and dominates over the other two; and just in proportion as he gives himself up to the dominion of one of these loves and rejects the sway of the others he leads a consistent life. Society may assert that life is everything, and faith nothing, when it talks abstractly; but its common sense ever shows more wisdom by transferring the quality of the motive to the act, as often as it finds any clew to the knowledge of motive. Of course, society makes many blunders in these judgments, because it reads the heart of man very imperfectly; but the nature of man leads him constantly to attempt penetrating the heart before forming his opinion of an action.

There is no need of restricting the word creed to the forms of faith adopted by particular churches. Whatever a man believes is his creed, and every man has a creed, however much he may be opposed to forms of faith; and this creed is the rule of his life, however strongly he may assert, and however implicitly believe, that faith is of no importance. Take, for instance, a man who devotes his whole energies to the pursuit of riches from a conviction that they are the greatest good this world affords. If he have large caution, he will take care not to break the laws of the land; but everything short of that he will do to attain his loved object. Perhaps he has large love of approbation; he will then be a little more cautious, and will do nothing that can injure his reputation as a gentleman; at least unless he believes that what he does will not be known in society. Perhaps, however, he has neither of these restraining traits, and is of a violent disposition; he will then be ready to rob or murder, if such means seem to promise to give him his desires. Shall we say this man has no creed, when his faith in the value of riches impels him to devote body and soul to the acquisition of gain? Does not his creed run thus: "I believe in gold as the one great good, and for this will I sacrifice all else that I possess." And does not his life and death devotion to this creed put to shame the feeble efforts of many of us who believe that we devote ourselves to more worthy ends?

So it is with those who employ themselves exclusively in the attainment of intellectual wealth. Faith that this is the one great good incites them to unwearied labor,—causes them to forget food, sleep, friends, everything, in order that they may acquire abundant stores of learning; and all because they have taken as their creed, "I believe that learning is better than all beside, and for this will I labor day and night."

So it is with the ambitious man. Who labors more devotedly than he; ever keeping his creed in mind, "I believe that power and reputation are above all other possessions, and to gain them I will sacrifice time, labor, truth, and justice."

So it is with every man and every woman the world over. The slothful even—those who seem impelled to nothing—refrain from effort because they put their faith in idleness as the one thing above all others desirable.

Mankind are possessed of Understanding no less than Affection; and by this, their inherent nature, they are compelled to believe no less than to love. It is vain to talk of cultivating the Affections that charity may be perfected in humanity, and at the same time omit all care of the faith. The mind will and must believe so long as it continues to think; and it is as unsafe to leave it without cultivation as to abandon the heart to the instruction of chance. The question is not, shall we or shall we not adopt a creed; for however strongly we may resist, we cannot refrain from holding one; but, what creed shall we adopt? Accordingly as we answer this question so will the measure of bur wisdom be both here and hereafter.

The human race may, in this respect, be divided into three classes,—those who adopt good creeds, those who adopt evil creeds, and those who, too indolent or too heedless distinctly to adopt any rule of life, spend their days in vascillating between the two; but the latter, by reason of the greater tendency to sin than to holiness inherent with the human race, tend, year by year, more and more decidedly towards the evil.

It is impossible that any person should lead a consistent life unless a creed be adopted and steadfastly acted upon; because unless one holds distinct opinions in relation to life and duty, one is drawn hither and thither by impulse and passion, as the mind's mood varies from time to time, so that the words and actions of to-day will be often in direct opposition to those which were yesterday, or which will be to-morrow.

In order to lead a life worthy an immortal being, a child of God, the first step to be taken is to come to a distinct understanding of what one wishes to be and to do. The biographies of those who have distinguished themselves in the world, either for goodness or for greatness, frequently show that in early life they adopted certain modes and directions of effort, and have attained to eminence by steadily persevering in one direction. Among the papers of these persons, written rules have been found which they have laid down for themselves as creeds, and in harmony with which they have built up their Characters; and herein lies the secret of their success.

The living in accordance with such creeds will not insure greatness or distinguished reputation, because after all our efforts, no one can be sure of worldly and external success. Events which it was impossible to provide for, or even to foresee, will often confound the best preparations of humanity, because the providence of God overrules all the events of life, according to the eternal dictates of infinite wisdom and mercy,—a wisdom that knows when it is best for us to succeed and when to fail in our wishes and endeavors, and a mercy which, looking to our eternal welfare, sometimes makes us sorrowful here that we may the more rejoice hereafter.

Perhaps the cause which most frequently prevents the adoption of a creed is the failing to recognize the seriousness of life in this world. Few persons can be found so senseless or so reckless as not to recognize the seriousness of death. Probably few could look upon the solemn stillness of the lifeless human countenance without a feeling of awe at the thought that ere long their day too must come when the beating of the busy heart shall cease, and the now quick blood shall stay its course,—when the hand shall lose its cunning and the brain its power. Such impressions are too often transitory, passing away with the object that awoke them, because persons do not stop to consider why it is that solemnity and awe pervade the presence of death. If they did, they would feel that this solemnity was reflected upon life, and life would became to them serious as death. Both would be serious, but neither sorrowful; for then death would lose its terror and would be looked forward to simply as the beginning of eternal life. The solemnity of life lies in the fact that it is a preparation for eternity; and the solemnity of death in the fact that the preparation is over and the eternity begun. In all this there is no cause of sadness, but infinite cause for thoughtful seriousness.

When the true solemnity of life is comprehended, and the Character is moulded in accordance with the ideas that in consequence possess the soul, a growth of the whole nature is induced that prevents all the repulsive characteristics of old age. Too often old age is utterly disagreeable through the indulgence of ill-temper, fretfulness, and selfish indifference to the wishes and pleasures of the young. Such traits of Character could never possess us if the true import of life were comprehended, and the Character formed in harmony with its teachings. A Character that grows in grace daily must become more and more beautiful and attractive with advancing years. Each day, as it finds it better fitted for heaven, must find it less sullied by the imperfections of earth.

We sometimes see persons discontented and peevish because they are old,—because they feel that they must soon pass away from the earth. Could this be, if they believed that life on earth was only a preparation for an eternal life in heaven? Could they shrink with aversion at the thought of death if they believed it to be the portal of heaven? The follies and the vices, the weariness and the sadness, the discontent and the moroseness of life, all spring from the want of a just conception of its relations and its value, such as can be attained only by calm, deliberate reflection, out of which wise opinions evolve, and are gradually shaped into a creed such as forms the bone and muscle of a wise and noble Character.

Evil is ever the result of the abuse of some good; for nothing was created evil. The narrow creeds of various churches, by which men's souls have been unworthily bound, have sprung from the falsification of the fact that man requires faith in truth that he may be able to lead a life of goodness. Had the makers of these creeds gone directly to the Bible for their materials, instead of looking into their own minds,—had they been content to accept the Ten Commandments given to the Jewish, or the Two given to the Christian Church, much mischief might have been avoided; but, not satisfied with the simplicity and directness of God's word, they built up creeds from their own minds, not as guides to a holy life, but as chains to compel the minds of other men into harmony with their own. Just in proportion to the energy with which they strove to impress themselves upon the people through these creeds was their indifference to that life' of holiness which should be the end of all creeds.

The centuries that have passed since the Christian dispensation was proclaimed have many of them been darkened even to blackness by insane endeavors to write creeds of man's devising, in letters of fire and blood, upon the nations. The day for such deeds has passed away from most lands calling themselves Christian; and now men are inclining to rush into the opposite extreme, and to mistake licentiousness in belief for liberty of conscience. Such an extreme naturally follows the opposite one that preceded it; but out of the anarchy of faith that now prevails the providence of God. will surely, in his own good time, lift up his children into the liberty wherewith those who obey him are made free. Then will it be understood that the truth is not a chain to bind the soul, but a shining light illuminating all the dark places of the earth, and pouring into every soul that worthily receives it a living warmth, that shall clothe the whole being with the beautiful garments of heavenly charity. Then shall it be seen that all true creeds are contained within the two commandments of the Son of God. Thou shalt love the Lord with all thy heart and soul and mind and strength; and thy neighbor as thyself.

IMAGINATION.

Imagination rules the world.

—NAPOLEON.

Imagination is the mediatrix, the nurse, the mover of all the several parts of our spiritual organism. "Without her, all our ideas stagnate, all our conceptions wither, all our perceptions become rough and sensual."

—FEUCHT ERSLEBEN.

Imagination is that power of the mind by which it forms pictures or images within itself. Thought is but a shapeless, lifeless entity, until Imagination moulds it into form. We cannot bring what we know out into life until Imagination presents it to the Affections as a possible reality. Thought is an uncreative power, and gives form to nothing. Imagination is a more positive power, and can impart form to everything in thought. Thought acts subjectively, while Imagination is more objective in its operations. Thought is, by itself, a pure abstraction: passing into the Imagination it becomes a possible reality, and in the Affections a vital reality. The Affections cannot love or hate anything while it is a mere Thought; but when it becomes an image, it is at once an object either of attraction or repulsion. Thought, therefore, can be lifted up into the Affections, and then be made manifest in life, only through the medium of the Imagination.

It has been remarked by a celebrated writer, that all great discoverers, inventors, and mathematicians have been largely endowed with Imagination. It might with equal truth have been added, that all successful persons in every department of life are endowed with an Imagination commensurate in power with that of the other faculties. To the mechanic in his shop, no less than to the student in his cell, is it requisite that he should be able to form a distinct image in his mind of whatever he wishes to perform. So the teacher, the preacher, and the parent labor in vain unless there is clearly imaged in their minds the end to be attained by education and discipline. It is idle to seek for means to accomplish anything until there is a distinct image in the mind of the thing that is to be done. If there be such a thing as an "airy nothing," it is a thought before Imagination has given it a "local habitation and a name." When Shakespeare said it was the office of the poet to carry on this transformation, he announced one of those great general facts which are equally true of every other human being. It is in degree, and not in kind, that one man differs from another. In this, the poet is but the type of what every human being must be, if he would be anything better than a dead weight in society, incapable of success in any department of life.

Let no one fold his hands supinely, and say, I have no Imagination; and therefore, if this doctrine be true, my life must be a failure. You may possibly have but one talent while your neighbor has ten, but you are just as responsible for the cultivation and enlargement of your endowment as your neighbor for his. Had the parable been reversed, and had he who was endowed with five talents hidden them in the earth while he who had one doubled his lord's money, the condemnation and the acceptance would likewise have been reversed. Unless a man be so far idiotic that he is not an accountable being, we blaspheme the goodness of God, if we say there is nothing he is capable of doing well.

The action of the Imagination may be best illustrated by example. Previous to the days of Columbus, many sea-captains believed that there was a Western Continent; but their belief was a cold faith, existing only in Thought. When the ardent mind of Columbus received the same belief, Imagination speedily formed it into a reality of such distinctness that faith changed to hope, and then Affection brooded upon it until his whole being was absorbed by the determination that he would be the discoverer of this unknown world. The image of this land was a pillar of cloud by day and a pillar of flame by night, leading him onward in spite of every discouragement and disappointment. Others might lose their courage, or die of weariness by the way; but his was that deathless enthusiasm that knows neither despair nor doubt. To this intense Imagination the world owes a new continent, and it is to such Imaginations that it owes almost, if not quite, all the great discoveries and inventions that have ever been made. There are those who love to believe that such things are in the main the result of accident; but it is only to the thoughtful and the imaginative that accident speaks. To the dull and the indifferent it is utterly dumb.

What is life but one long chain of accidents, if by accident we understand all that falls out without our own intention or volition. We cannot control these accidents. There is a power above circumstance and accident that controls them, as gravitation controls the motions of material things. We can only turn them at our will, and make use of them, as the machinist turns the power of gravitation to serve his purposes.

Quick-witted persons are those who have the power of rapidly seeing the relations of things in every-day life,—whose Thoughts grasp, and whose Imaginations shape with dextrous rapidity, the little accidents of the hour, and turn them to advantage. Persons of resource are those who have a deeper Thought, a more earnest Imagination; and who can therefore lay hold of great principles, and unusual circumstances, with a power adequate to meet great 'emergencies, and to make use of great opportunities. If we trample sluggishness and indifference under our feet, if we do with a will whatever we undertake, determining to do it as well as we possibly can, we shall become quick-witted in small works, and full of resource in large undertakings.

The Imagination is often talked of as if it were a useless part of our being, which should be put down and discouraged as much as possible; as if the Creator had endowed us with a power we did not need. So imaginative persons are spoken of with contempt, and here there is more justice; for, in common parlance, to be imaginative means to have the Imagination developed out of all proportion with the other powers. This is, perhaps, quite as bad as to have an insufficiency. What we should desire is a balance of powers. Imagination should not run away

53

with Thought and Affection, but neither should it lag behind them. All must act harmoniously and equally in a symmetrically developed Character. They are like the three legs of a tripod; and if either is longer or shorter than the others, or worse still, if no two are alike in length, the tripod must be an awkward and useless piece of lumber, instead of the graceful and useful article for which it was intended.

Whatever is to be done, from the discovery of a continent to the making of a shoe or a loaf, can be done well only by a person of Imagination. Go to a shoemaker and tell him exactly what you wish for a shoe, and it is your imagination that gives you the power of telling him so that he can understand your wishes. Every one can think, "I want a pair of shoes," but one must have Imagination to know what kind of shoe one wants, and a clear, distinct Imagination to be able to describe it intelligibly to another. Suppose you have this, and have told the shoemaker what you desire. Now, whether the man sends home to you a pair of misfits, quite different from those you ordered, or a pair just such as you want, depends in no small degree on his powers of Imagination. Any man can think enough to fasten materials together into the form of a shoe, and to make them vary in size according to a regular gradation of numbers; but this is all he can do unless he exercises his Imagination. Unless the image of a shoe, as you hold it in your Imagination, was transferred distinctly to the Imagination of the other, you will look in vain to find it translated into a material reality. So it is with your cook. She cannot make a nice loaf of bread, or prepare a dinner properly, by merely thinking as she works. The idea of a light loaf or of a well-cooked dinner must be distinctly in her mind, or you will eat with a disappointed palate.

It is needless to multiply examples here. We have but to look around us and see them everywhere.

Works of Imagination, of course, come in for their share of opprobium from those who, instead of striving to regenerate all the universal characteristics of humanity, would cut off and cast from it all those traits with which they least sympathize. In spite of their opposition, the mountain of fiction grows higher and higher every day, and the multitude throng its pathways to gather that food for the Imagination that is rarely given it in other compositions. Let the moralist talk and write against this as he may, it will be of no use, for the mass of human minds will never take an interest in any book that does not address itself to the Imagination. From the beginning of the world until now, no teacher and no writer was ever popular unless he addressed himself, in part at least, to the Imagination of the world.

When the Father of History read his nine books before the Greeks at the Olympic Games, and the people hung hour after hour and day after day upon his words, it was not merely because he glorified their victories that they listened with delight, but because he told the story with such vividness that every hearer beheld the on-goings of the tale pictured in his own Imagination. It was no dull recital of dry facts, the mere bone and muscle of History that he offered them, but the living story, the warm blood pulsating through it all, and every nerve instinct with life, In our own day, if the historian would forget the so-called dignity of History, which is but another name for lifelessness, and after having filled his mind with a clear, bright image of what he would relate, would present his story vividly to the Imagination of the reader, we should have no more complaints of the dulness of History. Who ever found Irving or Prescott dull? and yet they are accurate and faithful as the most stately and oracular. The carping critic may sneer at them because they are not philosophical and profound; but to have been read with delight by thousands who would never have reached a second chapter had they been other than they are, may well satisfy their ambition, and make them careless of the opinion of the critic. Such writers belong to the *Republic* of letters, not to that literary *Oligarchy* which insists that books should be written according to certain conventional rules which have been manufactured in the closet, instead of looking at the wants of the human mind, and then addressing themselves to those wants.

The class of minds that crave instruction for its own sake must always be very small; and it is this class alone that will read books in spite of their lack of imaginative power. Authors have no right to complain that their wise books lie unread by the multitude, if they persist in overlooking the nature of the human mind, and addressing themselves to what they think it ought to be instead of what it really is. They expatiate admiringly upon the simplicity and vividness of the style of Herodotus, and upon the classic taste of the Athenian public in appreciating him; and then, forgetting that the public of our own day are quick to admire the same traits, turn to their desks and write their histories as unlike as possible to him whom they have been praising.

The same repulsive want of Imagination too often characterizes Theology and Metaphysics, and prevents mankind from receiving the instruction from works on these topics that they need. In the early days of man's history, Religion and Philosophy addressed themselves to the Imagination, and then the people listened to their teachings; but gradually these heaven-born teachers turned more and more away from Imagination and towards Thought,—lost themselves in abstractions, dried up, withered, and changed into Theology and Metaphysics; and then the people turned wearily away from their words; and were they to blame? They wanted bread, and only stones were given to them. The multitude would not have followed the Lord, and listened with admiring wonder to his instructions, had they not been addressed to the Imagination. Infinite Wisdom clothed itself in parables, that the people might be instructed, and the people thronged to hear. The truths of Philosophy and Religion are of an interest more universal to humanity than the truths of all other science, for the first is to know one's self, and the second to know one's God; and yet the majority of teachers cover them with such a body of technicalities and abstractions, that it is vain for the mass of mankind to endeavor to penetrate to the soul within.

If the clergy of the Protestant Church would spend more strength in illustrating the Infinite Wisdom contained in the parables of the Lord, and less in amplifying the abstractions of St.

Paul, they would gather around them bands of listeners far more numerous and more devout than those that now attend their ministrations. It was one of the grand mistakes of that Church, at its first separation from the Romish, that, in its terror of the worship of material images, it passed into the opposite extreme of the worship of abstractions. This is one reason why Protestantism has made no advance in Europe since the death of the first Reformers, and why there is so little vital religion among the races by whom it was adopted.

Much has been done of late to render the natural sciences familiar and attractive to the popular mind, by lectures and books that bring them within the comprehension of all: and it is to be hoped, that, beginning thus with the material parts of the universe, mankind may be gradually led from matter to mind, from science to religion. The forms of external things are easily reproduced in the mind as images, and this is why natural science addresses itself more readily to the mind than any other branch of learning. When men learn to look within, and perceive that the things of the mind are as genuine realities as the objects of the external world, Philosophy will become attractive; and when the preacher warms Theology into Religion by abandoning the technicalities of abstractions for the living realities of piety towards God and charity towards the neighbor, he will rejoice in a listening audience.

The amount and the quality of that which we call originality, creative power, or genius, is entirely dependent upon the activity, force, and integrity of the Imagination. Talent belongs to Thought, and works only with facts and ideas as others have done before. It may be skilful, sensible, and faithful, but it can walk only in the old, beaten tracks. It can classify and arrange, but it can never discover or invent. Talent can understand and admire the mechanical powers; Genius puts them in harness, and makes them traverse land and sea to do his bidding. Talent loves to gaze on the fair forms of nature, and depicts them upon canvas with skill and truth, neither adding to nor subtracting from its model. Genius seizes upon the hints that nature gives,

57

and without being false to her, makes use only of that which helps to make up the beautiful, the sublime, or the terrible; showing the power that is within nature rather than nature herself. Talent sees life as it is, and so describes it, if it ventures into the domain of literature. Genius sees life as it is capable of being, and hence comes poetry and romance, depicting heroes and heroines, monsters and fiends, types rather than representatives of the human race. Talent perceives only the actualities of things, Genius their possibilities. Talent is content with things as they are, while Genius is ever striving to bring out latent capacities in whatever it deals with. If true to its higher impulses, Genius is ever striving to come nearer "the first good, first perfect, and first fair"; if false, it degrades and deforms everything it touches.

Mankind differ from each other in degree, but not in kind. By his power of thinking, a man has talent; by his power of imagining, genius. Quick-wittedness is genius in its lowest form,—genius applied to material life in its daily ongoings. The power for resource in emergencies is genius in a higher form. Invention—the putting together with an adequate purpose two things or ideas that never went together before—is genius in another form.

Admitting that men differ from each other, not in kind, but in degree, the question arises, Are all men capable of an equal degree of development? This may best be answered by comparison. All men are alike in the general conformation of their bodies; all have the same number of physical organs, designed for the same purposes. The relative power of these organs is, however, very different in different individuals. One has a fine muscular frame, and delights in exercises of physical strength, while effort of the brain is a weariness to him. Another has a finely developed brain, and delights in intellectual labor, while his strength of muscle is hardly sufficient for the absolute needs of life. One has the digestion of an ostrich, while another lives only by painful abstinence; and so on with indefinite variety. We know that much may be done by well-directed effort to overcome the weaknesses and imperfections of the body; but still

58

there is a limit to this, and all men cannot be strong and healthy alike. So it is with the powers of the mind. All men have the same number of powers,—this constitutes their humanity; but the relative force of their development varies in each individual. We know that a determined will works wonders in overcoming the defects of the body, and it can do more in overcoming the defects of the mind, because the spiritual body of man is far more docile and flexible to the will than the natural body; but there must be limitations here likewise: still, progress is eternal, and no man can tell beforehand of how much he is capable.

In cultivating the powers of the mind, the first step is to admit distinctly to one's self the fact of human responsibility; to feel that we are stewards to whom the Lord has intrusted certain talents, and that we are responsible to him for the use we make of them. Indolence will perhaps tell us that we are of very little consequence, and that it is not worth while for us to trouble ourselves about developing our understandings; that it is vanity in us to suppose that we can be of much use in the world; that we have but little leisure, and may as well amuse ourselves with books and society; for we need recreation, wearied as we are with the cares of life. Let us answer each of these excuses by itself; and first, we are of so little consequence. If the tempter take this form to slacken your efforts, tell him you are one of God's children, and therefore, by your birthright, of eternal consequence; that he who is faithful in the least things thereby proves his capacity for being faithful in much, and that by showing your willingness to serve the Lord in the small things of life, you are fitting yourself for serving him in large things, if not in this world, yet in the world to come. Moreover, is not every one of the highest consequence to himself; and is not the least of human beings as much interested to save his own soul as the greatest? Then, as to use in this world, you are responsible to the fullest extent of your abilities for the influence you exert in your sphere as entirely as is the greatest of human beings in his. No one is so small that he brings no influence to bear upon the social circle; no one so insignificant that he does not exert an influence, even by the expression of his countenance, though he may speak no word. Where can we find a circle that is not shadowed, as by a cloud, if one countenance appears within it darkened by sullenness, ill-humor, or discontent? Where one that is not warmed and cheered, as by a sunbeam, if one enters it whose features glow with good-humor, contentment, and satisfaction? Then does not the command to love our neighbor make us even responsible for the expressions our faces wear? In relation to the plea for recreation and amusement, it can readily be shown how these may be made subservient to a true and high cultivation of the understanding. While few are slow to admit our accountability in all that relates to the cultivation of the Affections, many seem to suppose, that in what relates to the Understanding we may, without wrong, follow our own inclinations. This opinion comes from a false estimate of the nature and uses of the Understanding. If considered as a mere receptacle for Latin and Greek, Mathematics and Metaphysics, Science and Literature, we may, without moral turpitude or virtue, abstractly considered, follow our own inclinations; but the Understanding will all the time be growing either stronger or weaker, wiser or more foolish, whether we study them or whether we let them alone. This action of the Understanding cannot go on without influencing the Affections. The one is as much the gift of God as the other, and each alike demands a healthful nutriment. An Understanding whose attributes are ignorance and folly can never promote a healthful growth of the Affections.

It has been already said that the Understanding of a great majority of human beings can be reached only through its imaginative side. Every one who is accustomed to children knows that this is universally true of them. Tell a child an abstract truth, and it falls dead upon his ear; but illustrate the same truth in a little story, and he is quick to estimate its justice. This continues true of most persons during their whole lives, so that it is vain to attempt touching their minds in any other way than by presenting them with some image illustrating the truth inculcated. Those who are capable of receiving an abstract truth without such an image are frequently so from the fact that the moment such a truth is presented to their Understanding, their Imagination is prompt to furnish the corresponding image. Unless this is done either by the speaker or the listener, the truth is apt to be only a useless piece of lumber stored away in the thoughts. The whole secret of the fascinating power of the novelist lies in his telling us of all that is most interesting to humanity, and presenting everything to the mind in images.

Most persons have so many duties to perform, that they have little time for voluntary employment, and then they want recreation, which, if they read, they say they can gain only through works of Imagination. There is nothing to object to in this, if such works be well selected and read wisely. There are many bad ways of reading novels; but there are two to be especially avoided; firstly, vitiating the Affections by reading impure novels; and secondly, weakening the powers of the Understanding by glancing through novels merely for the sake of the story. To read novels of doubtful or bad morality is as likely to corrupt the Affections as to associate with low and wicked companions. There is an abundant supply of pure and noble compositions of this sort on which the Imagination may feed without fear. If it morbidly craves the licentious pictures that come from the pen of such writers as Ainsworth or George Sand, its longings should be resisted as steadfastly as those which incline us to the gaming table or other scenes of licentious indulgence. On the other hand, the danger to the Understanding from skimming novels is far too much overlooked. It is not recreation, but dissipation, not a renewal, but a destruction, of the powers to read in this way. If you would be benefited by what you read, learn to read critically. Look at the characters, and see if they be natural and well drawn; observe the morality, and see if it be true or false; examine the style, and see if it be good or bad, graceful or awkward, distinct or vague. Novel-writing is one of the fine arts, and by looking upon it as such, you may cultivate your taste and discrimination to an extent you little dream of.

Imagination is the marriage of Thought and Affection, and the Fine Arts are its first-born children, and represent humanity in all its phases more fully and truly than any other department of art or science. What we know as the useful arts, which are born of man's love for physical ease and pleasure, are of comparatively modern date; but history goes not back to the time when the mind of man first took delight in fashioning and admiring the products of the fine arts. Many suppose them God-given and coeval with the birth of man. Music, painting, sculpture, poetry, and romance are the five departments of the fine arts. When these are studied and loved merely for amusement, they are of little or no use; if they are made vehicles for filling the mind with impure and evil images, they are shocking abuses; but if they subserve pure and holy purposes, elevating the soul towards all that is beautiful and good, they are true Apostles of the Word. Their ministrations are almost if not quite universal. It would be hard to find a human being whose soul is not stirred by one or other of them.

Comparatively few persons have it in their power to enjoy the delight and the refining influence that are derived from the highest exhibitions of skill in those departments of the fine arts that address themselves to the eye and the ear; but poetry and romance, the most intellectual and the most varied of them all, are accessible to every one. As those blessings that are far off and difficult to be attained are usually those which are most highly prized, we often find persons sighing for the culture to be obtained from music, painting, and sculpture, and overlooking or undervaluing the higher culture to be derived from poetry and romance. The best gifts of Heaven are always those which are most universal. Let any one read the plays of Shakespeare, the poems of Milton, and the novels of Scott carefully and critically as he would study a gallery of pictures, and he will find his taste refined and elevated as much as it could be by a visit to the Vatican. The genius of these authors is to the full as high and noble and original as that of Raphael, Angelo, or Titian. The means of culture are not far-fetched and dear-bought. They lie around us everywhere, and to make use of them is a luxurious recreation of the mind. What mother, wearied and worn by the cares of maternity, what laborer, exhausted with toil, what student, faint with striving for fame, but would be refreshed and renewed for the warfare of life by forgetting it all for a little while in the realms of the ideal world?

The common, vulgar misuse of novel-reading by the silly, the empty-headed, and the corrupt, should not blind us to its benefits. There are those who in music, painting, and sculpture find only nutriment for sensuality and impurity. Shall we, therefore, deny to all, and banish from the world the refining ministrations of beauty in form and color and sweet sounds? As justly may we wage war upon the wayside flowers because the children are now and then tardy at school from stopping to gather them. The Creator could never have strown beauty broadcast upon the face of the earth if it had no use. The very abundance of this nutriment offered to our love of beauty is evidence of its value; the very fact that we can abuse this love so fearfully is proof of its capacity for elevated usefulness.

Reading good works of Imagination in the thoughtful way that has been described will be very likely to rouse an action in the mind that will make it crave something more solid; and all should learn, if possible, to love instructive books. The brain that is overtasked by muscular labor—for the nervous energy of the brain is exhausted by physical effort as well as by mental—is the only one that is excusable for refreshing itself only with images from the ideal world. There are Sabbaths of rest to all sometimes, when opportunity may be found to gain something of a more nutritious quality; when, through biography we may learn to know some good and great character that will ever after stand in the mind an image of excellence to cheer us on our way, and make us feel with joy that there is power in us to do likewise; or perhaps some book of science that will enlarge our ideas of the wisdom and goodness of the Creator of us all. It should ever be remembered, that those whose minds are empty of images of goodness and truth are, almost of necessity, constantly becoming more and more full of images of evil and falsehood. Jealousy, envy, discontent, and love of scandal, are among the earliest products of an idle, empty mind. We are not, however, dependent upon, books for the means of cultivating the Imagination. There is a training of this power within itself, a morality of Imagination, that daily life compels us to observe if we would be practical, moral beings.

The first requisites in a healthy, well-developed Imagination are truth and distinctness. To those who deem Imagination but another name for fiction and falsehood, it may seem a contradiction in terms to talk of a true Imagination; but it is not so. Works of fiction charm us always in proportion as they seem true, and it is the morbid Imagination only that delights in falsehood. We sometimes see persons who, without apparent intention of falsehood, seem incapable of speaking the truth. If they relate a circumstance that has passed under their own observation, or describe anything that they have seen, they add here and diminish there, distort this and give a new color to that, in such a manner that the hearer receives an impression of nothing as it really is. If there seem to be no malicious or evil design in all this, such persons are commonly called very imaginative; they should be called persons of unregulated, unprincipled Imaginations. They do not bring Imagination under the sway of conscience, and their power of appreciating the truth will grow less and less until Imagination becomes a living lie.

Visionary persons form another class of those who do not regulate Imagination by the laws of him who is truth itself. With these, Imagination is as false in relation to that which is to come, as with the last described in relation to that which has already been. In their plans of life they reason from fancy instead of from fact, and their Imaginations are filled with fantastic visions of things impossible, instead of the clear, bright images of that, which may rationally be expected to come to pass. Such persons perpetually wasting their powers by trying to do so many things that they can do nothing well, or by striving to do some one thing that is impossible; thus rendering themselves comparatively useless in society, and often even mischievous. To avoid this error, it is needful to go back perpetually to Thought in order to obtain a solid foundation for Imagination to build upon. As Imagination passes to and fro between Thought and Affection, it must remember that it is a messenger from one to the other, and must not invent tales on the way, and so deceive Affection into acts of folly. The facts of the message must be precisely such as Thought gave them, while their costume may be such as Imagination would have it. Thus the Affections will be roused to action in proportion as the eloquence of the Imagination is more or less intense, When it speaks in "words that burn," if it speak from itself, it will rouse the Affections to wild fanaticism; but if it speak from Thought, it will waken enthusiasm in the heart, such as shall bear it steadfastly onward in the path of duty, "without haste and without rest." Distinctness of Imagination may be cultivated by carefully observing things we wish to remember, and then calling up their forms before the mind's eye, and endeavoring to describe them just as they are, in words, by writing, or by drawing; and then reexamining to see where we have erred, and correcting our mistakes. If this be done from a genuine love of truth, the Imagination will soon become accurate and trustworthy. In reading, strive to bring what is read before the mind's eye, and so impress it upon the memory in images. This process quickens the power of memory, and enables it to retain much more than it otherwise could. If the writer be imaginative, it is easily done; but if not, we must strive to make up for his deficiencies by our own efforts. Reading history and travels, constant reference to maps and pictures fixes facts upon the memory simply by transferring them to the Imagination. Memory is not a faculty by itself. What we only think about we remember feebly; what we image in our minds we remember much more strongly; what we love we never forget while we continue to love it.

In cultivating the Imagination, we must be sure to allow Thought to go with it hand in hand; remembering that the two together make up the Understanding. We must be careful to search conscientiously for true thoughts before allowing

Imagination to shape them into forms. In order to find the truth, we must love it for its own sake, and must seek it with straightforward earnestness, because we believe it needful to the building up of Character. If we seek it from any less worthy motive, our sight will become morbid, we shall lose the power of knowing it when it is found, and shall be liable to mistake for it some miserable falsehood. If we allow Imagination too much liberty, zeal will run before knowledge; if we allow it too little, knowledge will run before zeal. In the former, case we shall be liable to fanaticism; in the latter, to sluggishness. In the former case we shall be ready to undertake to do anything that attracts us, whether we know how to do it or not; in the latter, we shall not be willing to try to do what we might. The lack of Affection prevents us from desiring to do a thing, the lack of Imagination makes us think we cannot do a thing, the lack of Thought of course makes it impossible to do a thing; for we cannot do a thing till we know that it is to be done.

In our religion, Thought gives us faith, Imagination gives us hope, and Affection gives us charity. Religion does not become a personal matter to us until it takes the form of hope. While it is simply a thing of thought it is cold, barren faith, and we care nothing for it; but when Imagination touches it, faith is changed to hope, and we begin to perceive that religion is a thing to be desired in our own persons. Religious fear, too, is the child of Imagination. Devils believe and tremble, because they hate goodness. Angels believe and hope, because they love it.

Every one has within his mind an imaginary heaven, within and around which all cherished images arrange themselves, according as they are more or less dear. We should search our minds, and learn what are the attributes of our heaven, if we would know whether we are tending towards the true heaven that is prepared for those who order their lives aright. We shall, if we do this, be sure to find that there are certain images rising very often in our minds, into which our thoughts seem to crystallize when disturbed by no interruption from without; and these. images make up all that we believe of heaven; they are the kingdom of heaven within us. We may, with our lips, acknowledge faith in a pure heaven wherein dwelleth righteousness; but unless our ideas fall habitually into forms of purity, there is no genuine faith in such a heavenly kingdom. We truly believe only in what we love. We may learn from books and from instructors a great deal about the science of goodness, and may talk of such knowledge until we fancy that we should be happy in a heaven where goodness reigned triumphant; and yet we may be entirely deceived in this fancy, and our hearts may all the while be fixed on things so entirely apart from the true heaven, that nothing could make us more miserable than the being forced to dwell within its gates. If we would test the quality of our faith, we must watch the images and pictures that rise habitually before our mind's eye in our hours of reverie; for they faithfully represent the secret affections of the heart. If these images are forms of purity and goodness, it is well with us; the kingdom of heaven is truly there; but if they represent only forms of things that belong to this world, if dress and equipage and social distinction haunt our longings, if visions of pride, vain-glory, and luxury are ever prompt to rise,—visions that belong only to the love of self and of the world,—visions that do not beckon us onward to the performance of duty, but only entice us with the allurements of sensuality and self-indulgence; or still worse, if discontent, envy, and malice darken the temple of Imagination with their scowls, the kingdom of heaven is far from us as the antipodes. This imaginary heaven that selfishness and worldliness have built up within us is in truth but an emanation from hell. We may talk of heaven, and observe its outward forms all our lives while harboring this demoniacal crew within; and we shall grow ever harder and colder with intolerance and bigotry under their influence; nor can we ever have that joy in heavenly hope that belongs to those whose hearts cleave to all that is pure and true, and whose souls are therefore filled with the imagery of virtue.

We cannot expect, in this life, to attain to a state of regeneration so entire that no images of evil shall ever come to our souls; but we may hope to become so far advanced that we shall not welcome and entertain them when they come; but shall recognize them at once as often as they appear, and drive them from us. This much, however, we cannot do with our own strength, for that is weakness; but if we strive, looking ever to the Lord, whose strength is freely given to all who devoutly ask his aid, we shall be armed as with the flaming sword of cherubim, turning every way to guard the tree of life.

AFFECTION.

Love is the Life of Man.

—SWEDENBORG.

With the heart man believeth unto righteousness.

—ST. PAUL.

The Affections are the most interior of all the attributes of man,—they are in fact his spiritual life. The acquisitions of the Understanding truly appertain to man only when the Affections have set their seal upon them. We may store our memories with knowledge and wisdom gathered from every source, but until they are grasped by the Affections they do not belong to us; for till then they do not become part and parcel of ourselves. So long as we merely know a thing we make no use of it. The facts of knowledge, as they lie in the Understanding, may exhibit a rank growth of thoughts and images; but though flowers may adorn them, they will all perish barrenly; while, if the warmth of the Affections is thrown upon them, the rich clusters of fruit speedily appear; not only affording present delight, but promising to be the parents of numerous offspring yet to come.

The Affections cannot be analyzed and comprehended with the same kind of distinctness with which we comprehend Thought and Imagination; because that which belongs to the Understanding can be expressed or described in words, and in that form be passed from one to another; while the Affections exist only in forms of emotion that cannot be distinctly translated into words. A glance of the eye or a touch of the hand often transfers an emotion from one mind to another with a facility and clearness of which words are incapable. There are no things we believe so completely as those which we *feel* to be true, yet there are none about which we reason so imperfectly.

The motive-power in man is Affection. What he loves he wills, and what he wills he performs. Our Character is the complex of all that we love. We often think we love traits of

Character that we cannot possess; but we deceive ourselves. All that we truly love we strive to attain, and all that we strive after rightly we do attain. The cause of self-deception on this point is, that we think we love a certain trait of Character when we only love its reward; or that we hate other traits when we only hate their punishment.

The passionate man perceives that his ungoverned temper causes him trouble, and occasions him to commit acts of injustice, and to say things for which he is afterwards ashamed; and he exclaims, "I wish I could acquire self-control; but alas! a hasty temper is natural to me, and I cannot overcome it." Tell such a man that he is just what he loves to be, and he will deny it without hesitation; and yet the love of combating and of overcoming by force are the darling loves of his heart; and when he fancies that he is wishing to overcome these propensities, he is thinking only of the worldly injury his temper may occasion him, and not of the hatefulness of anger in itself. So soon as we begin to hate anger for its own sake we begin to put it away; but while we only hate the bad consequences of anger we cleave to its indulgence. So it is with indolence. We know, perhaps, that we are indolent, and we perceive that this vice stands in the way of our attaining to many things that we desire, and we believe that we wish to become diligent, when we are steadfastly loving a life of indolence, and wishing not for diligence, but for its rewards. What we suppose to be dislike of indolence is only dislike of the consequences that indolence brings in its train. So the drunkard sometimes goes to his grave cheating himself with the idea that the lust of the flesh binds and enslaves him; and that he really loves the virtue of temperance, while in truth he is loving sensual indulgence with all his heart. Possibly temperance reformers might be more successful in reclaiming such slaves from their sin if they would talk less of the punishments the drunkard brings upon himself in the shape of poverty, and disease, and shame, and enlarge more upon the moral degradation to his own soul which he fastens upon himself both for this life and the life to come.

We are all of us perpetually liable to gross self-deception by thus transferring in fancy our love or our hate for the consequences of vices or virtues to the vices or virtues themselves. If we made this transfer in fact, we should at once set about gaining the one and putting away the other; but so long as we believe that sin dwells within us without our consent and approval we become daily more and more the servants of sin.

We not unfrequently see a very poor family having an intense desire for education, and their poverty, instead of putting its acquisition out of their reach, seems only to stimulate their ardor of pursuit. One half of their time will perhaps be spent in the most arduous labor in order to procure the means of obtaining the aid of books and teachers to enrich the other half; and no self-denial in dress or physical indulgence seems painful, when weighed against the pleasure of increasing the means of education. Here is genuine love of learning, and the result of its efforts will prove the truth of the old adage, "Where there is a will there is a way." This family is acting out its life's love understandingly and with fixed purpose.

Perhaps in the very next house to this is another family of not nearly so small property. They too profess great love of and desire for education; but there is no corresponding effort. They must dress with a certain degree of gentility, and they must not make an effort to earn money by any means that would seem to lower their standing in society; and, moreover, they are indolent, and the effort that the denial of physical indulgences requires seems insupportable to them. The parents of this family will often be heard lamenting that their children cannot have an education; and if one should venture to indicate the possibility of their obtaining one for themselves as their neighbors are doing, they will reply that their children have not strength to struggle along in that way, or that they are too proud to get an education in a way that would seem to place them in point of social rank below any of their fellow-students. This family are acting out their life's love just as thoroughly, though not as understandingly, as the other. They do not desire education from love for it, but because it would give them a certain standing in society, and not having the means of indulging vanity in this direction, they turn to dress and idleness, as easier signs of what is vulgarly called gentility. Still these persons would deem you unjust and unkind if you told them they were living in ignorance because they had no true love for education; and they would hardly deem you sane should you tell them that the Character of every human being is the sum and continent and expression of all that he best loves.

We cannot truly love anything that we do not understand,—anything that has not a distinct existence in our thoughts and imaginations; and all of Character that we love and can clearly image to ourselves we can bring out into life. The Affections are the children of the Will, and if the Will be determined and steadfast, there is no limit but the finiteness of humanity to the progress in whatever is undertaken. When we love ardently, all effort seems light compared with the good we expect to derive from the possession of that which we love. If we become weary and faint by the way, it is because we lack intensity of love.

In reading the lives of distinguished men, we find that, in the pursuit of whatever has raised them above the mass of men, they knew no discouragement, acknowledged no impossibility. We read of travellers who, to satisfy a burning curiosity for discovery, pass through peril and fatigue that is fearful for us even to think of; and yet they, so intense was their love for what they sought, encountered all with a determination that made suffering and danger indifferent, nay, almost acceptable to them. So the inventor labors, year after year, through poverty and privation, compensated for all by the anticipation of the satisfaction that will be his when his darling object is attained. So the student, the philanthropist, the statesman, labors in like manner, lighted by thought, cheered by imagination, warmed by love. Needful as may be the light and the cheer, it is the warmth only that can give life. We may know and imagine, and yet perform nothing; but when love is wakened, performance becomes a necessity of our being; and every sacrifice of momentary pleasure we make in order to obtain the fruition of our desires is not only without pain, but it is sweet as self-denial to a lover, if perchance he may give pleasure thereby to the object of his passion. It is the merest self-delusion for any one to sit still and say, "I love this or I love that trait of Character; but it is not in my powder to gain it." They who love do not sit still and lament. Love is ever up and doing and striving. They who sit still and lament, love the indulgence of their own indolence better than aught else, and what they love they attain. .

It is of course impossible that all should become distinguished by the efforts they may make in life; and this is not what we should aim at in the training of Character. To be distinguished implies something comparative,—implies, if we aim after becoming so, that we seek to be superior to others. This is not an aim that can be admitted in Christian training. Character is something between us and our God, and every thought we admit that savors of rivalry or emulation in our efforts degrades them, and takes from them the sanctity that can alone insure success. The moment that finds us saying, "I am glad that I am better than my neighbor," or even, "I desire to be better than I wish to see him," that moment finds us destitute of a true conception of Christian charity. We cannot attain to a healthy growth of Character until, smitten by the beauty of excellence, we worship its perfection in our Lord and Saviour, and with hearts fixed on him, strive, trusting in his aid, to be perfect even as he is perfect. In this effort we must shut out from our hearts every emotion that cannot be admitted into our prayers to him for light and strength. Are we sorrowful that our neighbor is gaining upon the way faster than ourselves, let us remember that this emotion is virtually a prayer that his strength may be lessened for our sake; and let us change it as quickly as we can to a more earnest longing after our own growth, without comparing ourselves with any human being. Elation, if we think we have passed another in the race, is a vice of the same character as envy at another for surpassing us. Such envy and such elation are children of that pride of heart that shuts the door on all brotherly love. It is that vice by which Cain fell, and so far as we admit it into our bosoms we voluntarily become the children of Cain.

The Lord tells us to seek first the kingdom of heaven and its righteousness, and that all other good things shall be added unto us. We cannot suppose he meant by this that the reward of virtue was to be found in houses and lands, or worldly wealth of any kind, although he enumerated these things in the promise; for we know that these are, perhaps, as often possessed in abundance by the basest of men as by the most virtuous. How, then, are we to understand this promise? To seek the kingdom of heaven and its righteousness is to serve the Lord with all the heart, and soul, and mind, and strength; and the rewards appropriate to such service surely cannot be counted in silver and gold. These may adorn the happiness that virtue gives; but they cannot constitute it. He who labors simply for the love of wealth is content if he obtain the reward he seeks; but he who labors to obtain the fully developed character of a man,—the image and likeness of God,— if he attain nothing beyond wealth, would feel such reward to be only a mockery of his desires. Such labor lifts us above the happiness external possessions can give, and bestows upon us a wealth that the world cannot take away. He who wishes to serve God acceptably, cultivates all his capacities to the best of his ability, in order to increase his power of leading a useful life, and is therefore constantly adding to himself possessions that can never leave him;—rational and spiritual possessions which, in relation to our internal life, correspond to worldly possessions in relation to our external life, and were therefore signified in the parabolic language of the Lord.

When the philosopher of old lost the library he had been all his life-long collecting, he exclaimed, "My books have done me little service if they have not taught me to live happily without them." He had made their contents his own by diligent study, and no power could take this from him, and they had made him wise by their instructions, so that he could possess his soul in patience under external losses of any kind. The man who studies books, though he may not own a volume, makes them his own far more

74

completely than the bibliomaniac who spends a fortune in filling his library with choice editions of works life is not long enough to read. So it is with works of art. He who can most truly appreciate them is he who really owns them. One man will fill his house with pictures and statues and all beautiful works of art, because the possession of such things gives distinction in society. He collects them, not because he loves art, but because he loves himself; and values them precisely in proportion to the sums of money they have cost him. Those among his visitors who love art for its own sake, and have learned to appreciate such things justly, have a pleasure incomparably more interior and profound in gazing upon them than he who rejoices in having paid large sums of money for them; and surely no one of such visitors would exchange his power of appreciation for the others external possession of them. Who, then, is the true owner, if not he who feels most delight in contemplating them, and who has the most delicate perception of all their shades of beauty?

In the highest of all enjoyments of the eye, that which we derive from the contemplation of external nature, the man whose soul is most deeply thrilled by its beauty, whose heart rises in worship as he gazes upon the mountains in their calm sublimity, and remembers how the Lord frequented such heights for prayer, and who wanders beneath, the shadows of the woods, feeling that "the groves were God's first temples," this man surely has the kingdoms of the earth in closer possession than he who holds thousands of acres in fee.

Whatever possessions we can name, whether external or internal, whether of the heart, the head, or the hand, it is love by which we truly hold them. Nothing is ours that we do not love, and through love we obtain possession of all that our hearts crave.

The love, however, that is so strong to obtain must be no superficial sentiment, but an inward passion of the heart. So long as we live in thought and imagination we are very apt to mistake mere sentiment for love; but the difference will show itself so soon as we begin to act. Sentiment is soon wearied by labor and difficulty in its pursuit of mental attainment, soon disgusted by squalor or offended by ingratitude in its attempts at benevolence, soon discouraged by the hardness of its own heart when it endeavors to acquire self-control, or to gain such virtues as seem in the abstract lovely and delightful. In short, sentiment wants a royal road to whatever it strives to reach. Love, on the contrary, is too much in earnest to be dismayed by any impediment. It will not stop half-way and make excuses for its short-comings. It rests not in its course until it has gained what it seeks; and then it rests not long, for all true love "grows by what it feeds on," and every height of excellence we reach does but enlarge the field of vision and show us new countries to be won.

Admitting love to be, indeed, this intense and all-pervading power, and the very life of our souls, the importance of training ourselves to love only that which is pure and true at once becomes manifest. The heights of heaven are not farther from the depths of hell than are the results that come to us if we seek the pure and the true from those which inevitably occur when the choice falls upon the impure and the false. Let no one think to dwell in safety because he has not deliberately said to himself, "I choose the impure and the false"; for if the pure and the true be not deliberately and voluntarily chosen, the heart out of its own inherent selfishness and worldliness will unconsciously sink gradually, but surely, into the impure and the false. There is no half-way resting-place for humanity between good and evil. We are always sinking, unless we are rising; going backward, unless we are pressing forward.

Much is said of the truth and purity of childhood, and they are very beautiful, for the angels that care for children do continually behold the face of the Heavenly Father,—do stand perpetually within the sphere of absolute truth and purity. But soon the child slips the leading-strings of its guardian spirit, and comes into its own liberty; and now, unless it freely chooses to follow with willing and constant step in the same path wherein it has thus far been led, it will wander from side to side, increasing at each turning the distance that separates it from the way of life, until at last it may wander so far that it loses the desire and even

76

the memory which might lead it to return. Vicious propensities will, perhaps, begin to show themselves; and in the hardened and shameless youth it will be hard to recognize any trace of the innocence of infancy. But, perhaps, instead of viciousness, carelessness is developed, and youth is brightened by gayety, amiability, and ready generosity. Occasional derelictions from truth and honor find ready apologists among friends, because the boy or the girl is so "good-hearted"; but a closer inspection readily shows that the goodness of heart is very superficial, that the left hand is often unjust while the right is generous, that a lie is no offence to the conscience, if it be a good-natured one, and in short that very little dependence can be placed on the uprightness that has no firmer base than good-heartedness. Young persons of this sort are sometimes led away to commit some act so base that their eyes are opened to the dangers that beset the path in which they are travelling, and in sorrow and dismay they turn to seek the way of innocence whence they had wandered. Too often, however, the carelessness of youth passes into the indifference of adult life and the callousness of old age. What can be more revolting than an old age cold, hard, and selfish? Yet this is the natural and almost unavoidable result of a youth that does not fix its heart in unwavering love upon truth and purity,—whose aspirations are not for those things which cannot grow old, and which the world can neither give nor take away. A heart filled with love for excellence can never grow old; for it will go on increasing in all that is lovely and gracious so long as it lives; and where there is perpetual growth of the faculties there can be no decay. We grow old, not by wear, but by rust; and we can never become the prey of rust while our faculties are kept bright by the power and the exercise of earnest love. The fleshly body must grow old and die, for it is of the earth earthy; but it is by our own weakness and indolence if our spiritual body ever gathers a wrinkle on its brow. When the fleshly body drops from us, what must be our shame and our despair if we rise in a spiritual body deformed with evil passions, or corrupt with the leprosy of sin. Too many, alas! spend all their energies in feeding and clothing

77

and sheltering the natural body, leaving the spiritual body hungry and naked and cold. We sometimes hear wonder expressed that a mind thus starved has become super-annuated and doating, while the body still carries on its functions with vigor; but had the body been treated with a similar neglect, it would have long before returned to the dust. The growth of the spiritual body should be continuous from the cradle through eternity; and seldom can any other reason, than our own neglect, be assigned for its disease or decay. The bread of life is perpetually offered for its support, and if it refuses to eat, its death is on its own head.

Infants who pass into the spiritual world before they are touched by a taint of earth are, probably, through the absence of all evil in those who are suffered to approach them, trained into a purity of Affection that fills their whole being with its genial warmth, descending, or raying out, into all the imaginations of the soul and all the thoughts of the mind. Thus they serve God in the order which the Saviour commanded, with all the heart, and soul, and mind. They, however, who remain long on earth, almost without exception, have the order of their nature so reversed, that their powers must be converted to the right, in the order of St. Paul, ascending from the lowest to the highest; or, which is the same thing, passing from the outmost to the inmost. The lowest and most external part of the being must be made obedient to the laws of Divine Order, and on this as a foundation must the higher and internal nature be built up, until it forms a sanctuary; and upon its altar shall fire from heaven descend so often as a gift is offered.

The practice of external vice, just in proportion to its grossness, incapacitates us for perceiving what is true or loving what is good. By vice is not meant crime such as exposes us to punishment by the law of the land, but sins against the laws of God, that bring their own punishment with them, by defacing the image of God in the soul. There is always need of searching the heart to find if we have committed crimes against the soul; for the laws of the land deal only with the excessive derelictions from right which we cannot ignorantly commit. We may, however, go on unconsciously in the commission of great sins until our hearts become hardened against all emotions of heavenly affection, and our eyes blinded so that we cannot distinguish the difference between darkness and light. If we would avoid this fearful condition, we must often go to the Gospels, and place the words of the Lord, in their various teachings, especially as they come to us from the Mount, as it were in judgment over against us, and reading verse by verse, fathom the depths of our hearts, and confess whether we are guilty or no. Would we escape such guilt, we must study these instructions again and again, until, as Moses commanded of the laws of the elder Scripture, "they shall be with us when we sit in our homes, or walk by the way, or lie down, or rise up. And we shall bind them for a sign upon our hands, and they shall be as frontlets between our eyes. And we shall write them upon the posts of our houses, and upon our gates."

When we place the words of the Lord in judgment over against us, and feel compelled to acknowledge our unfaithfulness to their requirements, there is danger of our falling into despair through the consciousness that is thus forced upon us of our want of love for the law of the Lord. The indulgence of our own wills is so sweet to us, that we cannot see how it is possible that the yoke of the Lord can ever become easy to our stiffened necks. We feel as though an obedience that did not spring from true love could not be called obedience, nay, was almost a sin; for it seems to savor of hypocrisy. In this state of mind, our only refuge is in that faith which St. Paul tells us "is the substance of things hoped for, the evidence of things unseen"; and then, unless this faith be strong enough to make us obey, though not from love, yet from a simple belief that at any rate obedience is better than disobedience, our state is wretched indeed. Our rationality tells us that obedience is naught unless we love to obey, but an inward conviction of the soul—may we not call it the voice of God?— entreats us, saying, "this do, and thou shalt live." If, in the ardor of our faith, we can forget our rationality, and cry, "Lord, I believe; help thou mine unbelief"; and if we force ourselves to do that which we are commanded, though at first it may appear to us an act purely external and dead, we shall soon find, that, if planted in darkness, it is still a living seed, and the Lord will water it till it shall spring into a growth of beauty that our hearts will cleave to with delight.

The first obedience of the soul that has entered upon the way of regeneration is hardly less ignorant than that of the little child who obeys his parent without comprehending the use or propriety of his commands; and, like that of the little child, it consists in abstaining from doing that which is wrong, rather than in doing that which is right. As the child grows older, he can look back upon those commands and understand them; and then he is filled with gratitude and love towards his parent for putting them upon him. So he who seeks to love the Lord must obey first, and understand afterward,—must keep the commandments ere he can know the doctrines,—must abstain from doing wrong before the Lord can implant in his heart the love of doing right.

In the first stages of regenerating life we think we love the Lord, although we know that we do not love our fellow-beings as we ought; and we cannot comprehend the truth, that he who does not love his brother, whom he has seen, cannot love the Lord, whom he has not seen; and we think it is much easier to be pious towards God than to be charitable towards men. If our faith is strong enough to induce us to obey the external commandment of doing as we would be done by, the affection of true brotherly love by degrees grows up within us, we know not how, for the spirit of God has breathed upon us when we were not aware; and then we perceive how imperfect was the love we bore to the Lord, when we had not learned to feel that the attribute which awakens true love for him is the perfect love he bears towards each one of us, and that we can appreciate this love only so far as we imitate it by feeling willing to do all the good we can to every neighbor, without distinction of person, after the manner in which he causes the sun to shine and the rain to fall alike upon the evil and upon the good.

To live thus in charity with all men is not to do external acts of benevolence indiscriminately to all, without respect of person. There is a common, but erroneous, idea in the world, that simply to give is charity. To live what many esteem a life of charity, that is a life of indiscriminate giving, is often to pay a bounty upon idleness and improvidence, and to furnish the means of vicious indulgence. While remembering the command to give to those who ask, we must not forget the prohibition against casting pearls before swine. To give good things to those we have reason to suppose will abuse them is as wrong as to withhold our gifts from those who would use them. To give ignorantly, when we know not the value of the claim upon our benevolence, is at best but a negative virtue, and we should bear in mind that everything we bestow upon the unworthy is so much abridged from our means of aiding the worthy. Many persons seem to suppose that charity consists entirely in alms-giving, while this is only its lowest form. Kind deeds and kind words are as truly works of charity as pecuniary gifts, and we do not lead lives of charity unless we are as ready with those in the home circle and in our social relations as with these among the poor. God shows his love to his children by providing them with sustenance for the body, for the intellect, and for the affections, and if we would resemble him, we must show our love to the neighbor by being always ready to minister to the wants of those around us, in whatever form they may arise.

We are told to give even as we receive, and we are also told that we are stewards of the Lord; that is, that all our gifts are held in trust from him; and we must use them in such a way that at his coming he may find his own with usury. True charity never impoverishes. In outward possessions it would be hard to find a man who has made himself poor by acts of benevolence, for a just and wise benevolence is almost sure to be accompanied by an orderly development of the faculties such as in our country makes prosperity almost certain. In intellectual attainments most persons are familiar with the fact, that there is no way by which we can so thoroughly confirm and make clear in our own minds anything that we know, as by imparting it to another. In all that relates to the affectional part of our being, none can doubt that we grow by giving. The more we love, the more we find that is lovely; and it is only in proportion as we love that we can learn to comprehend that God is infinitely powerful by reason of his infinite love. If we would make our one talent two, or our five talents ten, the best way to do it is by giving of all that we have to those who are poorer than ourselves.

Every person has within him three planes of life, which constitute his being, and which, during the progress of regeneration, are successively developed; viz., the natural, the spiritual, and the heavenly. With those who lead an externally good life on the natural plane, that is, who act more from the impulses of a kind disposition or a blind obedience than from the light of Christian truth, charity consists merely in supplying the natural wants of the neighbor by making him more comfortable in his external condition; and this is well, for there is little, if any, use in trying to improve the inner man while the outer is bowed down with want or squalid with impurity. This is the basis of the higher planes of charity, the first in time, though lowest in degree. There are those who think lightly of this form of charity, because it is lowest in degree, forgetting that it is absolutely essential as a basis for everything that is higher. This truth may be illustrated by the duties of the parents of a family. It is easy to perceive that the highest duty of parents is the spiritual training of their children, that the second is to give them an intellectual education, while the third and lowest is to feed and clothe and shelter their bodies. This duty towards the body, although lowest in degree, is first in time; and ministering to the wants of the natural bodies of their children, that they may grow up strong and healthy, is the first duty to be performed in order to insure, so far as possible, a trustworthy basis on which to build up their spiritual bodies. It should, however, be distinctly kept in mind that this is only the lowest plane of parental duty, and that to rise no higher is, as it were, to lay a solid foundation with labor and expense, and then leave it with no superstructure, a monument of folly.

From this class of charitable persons come those who found institutions and lead reforms having in view the amelioration of the physical condition of the human race. In regarding this as the lowest class, no disrespect towards it is intended, for it is absolutely essential as a basis to the higher; but this foundation should be recognized as such by the founder in order that he may adapt it to the superstructure, and not elaborate the former at the expense of the latter. The parent may squander his means upon fine clothes and sumptuous fare until he has nothing left for the intellectual education of his children; the State may build palaces for the physical comfort of its paupers and criminals, until there is nothing left in the treasury to construct schoolhouses and colleges for the mental training of its virtuous children; the philanthropist may so bestow his charities that the recipient will learn to feel that it is the duty of the rich to support the poor, and so become a pauper when he might have been a useful citizen.

With those whose brotherly love is of the second, or spiritual, degree, charity is founded on the love of right, the love of giving to all their just due. Those of the first class will, perhaps, deem those of the second cold, yet a close observation will show that in the end more good is done to society through the efforts of the latter than of the former. Where the generosity of the first would reform the condition of a miserable neighborhood, by giving the sufferers food and raiment and shelter, the justice of the second would say all men should have the means of acquiring a support for themselves, and his efforts would be turned to providing employment, and encouraging a spirit of industry among the poor. Where the first would build almshouses and hospitals, the second would build factories and workshops. The first would lavish all that he had in direct gifts to the poor, and then have nothing more in his power to do for them, while the second, by husbanding his resources at first, would be able presently to place them beyond the need of aid. The first will be so generous today that it will be hard for him to be just tomorrow, while the second, by doing only justice now, gains power to bring about the most generous results hereafter.

This second degree of charity or brotherly love should not ignore or contemn the first, but build itself upon it. Justice must not forget mercy. The poor must not be suffered to starve before work can be provided for them, or they be taught to do it. One Christian virtue does not destroy that which lies beneath it, but rises to its true height by standing upon it. We do not pull away the base of a structure because we wish its top to be more elevated.

The third, or heavenly, degree of charity results from love to the Lord. This is the highest possible form of charity, and through its development man is brought into connection with the highest heavens. The first form of charity comes in great measure from a love of self. We obey its impulses because of our own personal distress at witnessing the distress of others; and where unrestrained by higher principle, these impulses often compel us to be unjust today because we were over-generous yesterday. The second form of charity results from true brotherly love, that leads us to restrain impulse because principle puts it in our power to do so much more for those who need our aid. The third form is the fruit of love to the Lord. It is warmer than the first and wiser than the second. It develops the whole power of man, both rational and affectional, by leading him to the eternal source of all power, whence cometh down to us all capacity to think and to love. Quickened by love to the Lord, we shall perpetually feel that we are his stewards, and while we are filled with gratitude towards him, as the giver of every good thing we possess, we shall equally be filled with desire to give even as we have received, good measure, running over, and shaken together. Then we shall feel, that, if we would lead lives of true charity, it must be by imitating the Lord, who showed forth his love towards his children, first by giving them the earth and all that it contained as an inheritance; secondly, by giving them the Word of his divine truth to teach them the way in which they should walk; and thirdly, by coming in person to show them the reality of a divine life. Finitely imitating this infinite example, as we advance in the regeneration of our Affections, we shall first give of our external possessions from the love of giving, and from a desire to make ourselves happy by seeing others so. Next, we shall give from the knowledge of truth that is in us, working with such wisdom as we possess, to help others to make themselves happy. Finally, love to God will lead us to perceive that charity in the highest degree is the leading a good life; and that he who is pure and holy and faithful is a living form of charity. While this state does not destroy, but fills full the two preceding ones it will perhaps diminish rather than increase the general action of the life upon society, because its tendency is to increase our earnestness in the performance of the immediate duties of life that are included in the family circle, and in all that relates to the particular occupation of the individual. This is the natural result of an interior love to the Lord; for this makes us feel his immediate presence in all the circumstances of daily life, and so causes us to look upon the duty that lies nearest as that one which the Lord wishes us to perform first; and till that is done, prevents our seeking out duties more remote and less apparent.

In studying the material manifestations of the Divine Love and Wisdom, we find that the perfection of each minutest part is a type of the perfection of the great whole. So in the material works of man, every whole thing approaches perfection just in the degree that its several parts are perfect; and it is vain to labor for great results while we overlook minute details. So in life, society can never be a virtuous and happy whole until each individual, in his special vocation, fulfils every duty pertaining to his station. If we would perform our quota of the great whole, we must, each in his place, fulfil the duties that lie around us; and we must beware how we go out of our way in pursuit of duty, unless we are confident that we are not neglecting, or perhaps trampling upon, a duty that lies directly in our path.

There is especial danger, at the present day, that many of us may need to be warned like the scribe of old, wearied with his task-work, not to seek great things for ourselves. As Baruch murmured because he must again and again write out the words of Jeremiah, so we cry out wearily at the daily recurring duties of life, and would fain seek some great thing whereby to show forth our devotion to the truth. This is because our love to the Lord is not yet strong enough to regenerate our Affections. In proportion as this is accomplished, duty will become lovely to us, because it is what the Lord sets before us to do. We all know how pleasant it is to do the will of those whom we most love on earth, and so would it be supremely delightful to us to do our duty if we had a similar love for our Father in Heaven.

As the little coral insect, obeying the blind instinct of its nature, adds particle to particle, and builds a house for itself at the same time that it helps to construct a continent; so we, obeying the voice of God, in every little duty, performed not grudgingly, but with the heart, are adding something to our eternal mansions, and helping to enlarge the bounds of heaven.

LIFE

"Thou shalt not respect the person of the poor, nor honor the person of the mighty: but in righteousness shalt thou judge thy neighbor."

—LEVITICUS xix. 15.

"There is but one thing of which I am afraid, and that is *fear.*"

—MONTAIGNE.

"Work! and thou shalt bless the day,
Ere thy task be done;
They that work not, cannot pray,
Cannot feel the sun.
"Worlds thou mayst possess with health
And unslumbering powers;
Industry alone is wealth—
What we do is ours."

Thought, Imagination, and Affection, combined harmoniously, constitute a symmetrical Character, and they should manifest themselves in an external Life of corresponding symmetry. The external Life will always fall short of the internal, because we can always imagine a degree of excellence beyond that which we have reached, let our efforts be earnest and active as they may; and the more we advance in Christian progress, the wider will the vista open before us of that which we may yet attain. As we ascend the heights of worldly knowledge, in whatever department, the horizon widens at every step; and we always know that the horizon, distant as it may seem, is only an imaginary limit to that which may be known. The shallow student, in the inflation of self-conceit, may fancy that his own narrow valley is the limit of the universe; but the wise man knows that limitation belongs only to his own organization, and not to the universe of God. So in the training of Character, we may go on in our progress, not only through time, but through the measureless periods of eternity, and yet we know that we can never reach that perfection of development which belongs to the All-perfect.

Among the insane dreamers of the earth, those are found who deem themselves enjoying light sufficient to live lives of perfection, even in this dim morning twilight that lies around us on earth; but it is their bat-like vision which takes for noonday that which, were their eyes couched, would seem to them but darkness visible. He who fancies that he leads a perfect life is but a dreamer concerning things of which he has no true knowledge.

Perfection is, nevertheless, the object at which we should patiently and steadfastly aim, and the loftiness of the mark, unattainable though it be, will shed an ennobling influence on those who strive. The mass of human beings aim at nothing higher than to be as virtuous as, or a very little more so than, their neighbors; and are often more than contented when they think they have reached the low mark at which they aim. To compare ourselves with our fellow-beings is always dangerous, and leads to envyings, rivalries, pride, and vainglory. In all our aims, the absolute should be our only mark. If in intellectual pursuits we strive only to know as much as our neighbors for the sake of decency, or to know more than they for the gratification of pride, or for the pursuit of wealth or honor, we shall never reach so high a point as if we studied without ever stopping to compare ourselves with any one; but worked right on, incited simply by the desire of knowing all that our capacities and opportunities would enable us to acquire. Working thus, we should go on our way rejoicing, our hearts embittered by no envyings, inflated by no conceit. Comparing what we know with that which we do not know, we could never become vain of our acquirements, for we must always feel that what we know is but the beginning of that which remains to be learned.

So in Life, if we compare our own lives with the lives of our neighbors, we shall be envious and jealous, or else self-conceited and proud; and our efforts will probably soon slacken, and then cease; and then we shall begin to go down hill, at the very moment, perhaps, when we are taking credit to ourselves for our rapid, or our finished, ascent. If, on the other hand, we compare our lives with that absolute perfection which the Lord sets before us as our model, we shall incur the danger of none of these vices; and though the greatness of our task may well cause us to "work in fear and trembling," we shall ever be cheered by the consciousness that "the Lord worketh within us both to will and to do."

When our characters take form in external Life, Thought must give us discrimination, Imagination must give us courage, and Affection must give us earnestness; then our external nature will be the transparent medium through which the internal nature will shine, with a lustre undiminished by the opacity which is sure to dim its radiance when dulness, fearfulness, or indolence inheres with the external nature; for then it forms a husk to hide, instead of a medium to display, the workings of the inner being.

The powers that have been treated of in the preceding essays are sometimes found to work well so long as they work upon abstractions; but so soon as they are required to work upon the daily Life, they fail of reaching so high a point of excellence as we think we had reason to anticipate. This results from the want of either discrimination, courage, or earnestness; and the inner nature cannot be thoroughly trained until these faculties are so developed by its life-giving power, that their weakness ceases to interfere with its movements when it seeks to manifest itself in external Life.

Thought can discriminate abstractions long before it can discriminate facts in their relations with Life. It can reason logically of the true and the false in the realms of the mind long before it can tell the right from the wrong with correctness and readiness in the daily ongoings of events. To discriminate justly here, we must be able to dissipate the mists with which the love of self and the love of the world obscure the way in which we tread; hiding that which we *ought* to love, and displaying in enlarged proportions the things that we *do* love, until reason loses all just data, and accepts whatever passion offers as foundation for its judgments. Persons thus misled, often think they really meant to walk steadfastly in the right path, and that they are not responsible for having wandered into the wrong. They call what they have done an error of judgment, and rest content in the belief that their intentions were good, and therefore they are not to blame. This may be true, for "to err is human," and none but the All-wise can be sure of always judging rightly. Still, when we know that we have done wrong through an error of judgment, we should carefully examine and see if we might not have avoided this mistake had we been more careful in our investigation of facts,—more conscientious in our process of adopting our opinions. If we thus catechized our past errors, we should probably find, that, in a large proportion of cases, our error sprang from some cause we might have prevented,—from carelessness, from blindness caused by the desire to gratify our own wishes, or from indolence; in fact, that what we fancied sprang from an error of judgment only, had a much deeper root, and drew its nourishment from undisciplined Affections.

In training the faculty of discrimination, the work we must set before ourselves is to learn the relative value of principles, of persons, and of things; and in order to do this, we must look upon them in their relations with time and with eternity. We must learn to value and to judge from laws of absolute right, and not from the expediencies of the hour.

Protestants quote with horror the Romish maxim, that, "for a just cause, it is lawful to confirm equivocation with an oath," yet the same principle lurks within their own bosoms, inciting many a well-intentioned soul to "do evil that good may come of it." The two maxims are twin sisters, and children of the father of lies. Persons who think they have delicate consciences not unfrequently tell what they call small lies, or lies of expediency, in order that some good may come of it, which they

90

esteem so great that it overbalances the evil of the falsehood. This class of persons is very numerous, and of all degrees, running from the mother who deludes her child into being a "good boy" by the promise of punishment or of favor that she has no intention of bestowing, to the juror who swears to speak the truth, and then affirms that a guilty man is innocent, fancying that it is less a sin for him to commit perjury than for the powers that be to commit what he calls oppression, injustice, or legal murder. This willingness to commit one sin, in order to prevent our neighbor from committing another, is a form of brotherly love we are nowhere enjoined to practise; it springs from an overweening self-love, that believes itself too pure to be contaminated by a small sin, while it forgets that a wilful disobedience of one commandment is in its essence disobedience towards the whole law. All who do evil that good may come of it, in any department of life, belong to this same class of persons. They ever look upon the sins of their neighbors with a sharper eye than they turn upon their own; and ever hold themselves in readiness, by "righteous indignation," intemperate zeal, and wisdom beyond, that which is written, to do battle for the Lord with weapons he has forbidden us to use, and to set the world in order by means and principles in direct opposition to his laws.

No one could be guilty of such sins who possessed a discriminating sense of right and wrong; such a sense as is derived from receiving the teachings of the Lord in simplicity of heart, and never presuming to set aside his commandments in order to place our own in their stead. His commands to refrain from doing evil are explicit, and without reserve, and he who ventures to call in question their universal application is sharpening a weapon for the destruction of his own soul.

The commands of the Lord are infinite principles, and in their natural and simple deductions cover all the acts of Life having any moral bearing, from the greatest to the least; and it is not the wisdom, but, the foolishness, of man, not his depth, but his shallowness, that endeavors to limit their significance and their application. We shall find that our vain attempts to do this occasion almost all our errors of judgment. "The testimony of the Lord is sure, making wise the simple," and he who is implicitly guided by it can alone walk surely; for he only has an unfailing guide in his endeavors to distinguish accurately between right and wrong.

If we learn to discriminate principles wisely, our next step is to apply a similar action of the thoughts to persons; and here again it is to the laws of absolute good and evil we must look for light. We must learn to respect persons for what they are, and not for their position, their reputation, or their worldly possessions. If we are really aiming to train our own characters in accordance with the laws of absolute right, we shall be likely to respect in others the attributes we seek in our own persons. In all other efforts, there is too often envy and jealousy among those who strive; but with those who seek true excellence, whether intellectual or moral, *for its own sake*, and not from love of the world, there is always pure brotherly love; and a perpetual delight is experienced in the contemplation of excellence wherever it is found.

In our estimate of the relative value of things, the same laws are called into action. If we would value them aright, we shall seek first those which aid us in improving and educating our characters, or which enlarge our powers of usefulness, and be comparatively indifferent to things which are external, and contribute only to the pleasure of the hour.

True discrimination may be defined as the faculty by which we justly estimate the value and the relations of principles, of persons, and of things; and so far as we attain to it, the power of wise Thought is ultimated in Life.

Courage, the buoyant child of Imagination, is the next faculty which we must duly cultivate, if we would use the talents God has bestowed upon us to the best advantage. It is common to look upon courage as a natural endowment, and few persons seem to be aware that it is a moral trait we are bound to cultivate. Yet when we consider how the want of courage interferes with our powers of usefulness, we cannot doubt that conscience should have force to make brave men and women of us all. In the various relations of life there is nothing that so paralyzes the powers as fear. They who are the subjects of fear are slaves, let their position or their endowments be what they may. The want of courage in practical life brings failure, casualty, and even death, in its train: intellectually, it robs us of half our power; morally, it puts us in bondage to our fellow-beings; and religiously, it leaves us without hope.

Hope and fear are alike children of the Imagination; but how different is their aspect! Fear walks through the world with abject gait, searching constantly after something of which it may be afraid; for, like all the other faculties, it perpetually demands food, and if it finds it not in the world around, imagines it in the world within. Few persons, perhaps none, are fearful in every department of life; but almost every one is so in some particular relations. Just so far as we succumb to fear, we lose the control of our powers, and lie at the feet of circumstance instead of cooperating with it, and making it subserve our benefit. Hope, on the contrary, finds cause for joy everywhere, and when surrounded by gloom sees, in imagination, the dawn that must come even after the blackest night, and is buoyed up by the remembrance, that, though "sorrow may endure for a night, joy cometh in the morning." Where fear sees nothing but the black clouds that threaten coming storms, hope looks through them to the bow of promise. Hope is the internal principle of true courage. St. Paul, in his beautiful description of charity, tells us that it "hopeth all things"; and we may easily perceive how it must be so, for the external form of charity is love to the neighbor, which leads us to hope all things for our fellow-beings; while its internal form, which is love to God, must lead us to hope all things for ourselves. The devils believe and tremble because they hate God; the devout believe and hope because they love him.

Let us consider courage specially in its four principal relations,—physical, intellectual, moral, and religious.

Physical courage,—the courage of practical life,—though it seems the lowest form of this virtue, is perhaps quite as rare as

93

either of the others. There is abundance of fool-hardiness, of brutal rashness, indifferent to all consequences, in the World; but very little of that calm, self-possessed courage that leaves to one the full use of his faculties in the midst of danger, and allows him to act wisely, even when meeting death face to face. The only sure foundation for this form of courage is unshrinking trust in the overruling power of God,—a trust that shall make us feel his providence ever clasping its arms about us in all the circumstances of life, causing us ever to bear in mind, that he who watches the fall of the sparrow cannot permit us to perish or to suffer by chance. This trust will give us power to meet the prospect of death with calmness, let it threaten in what form it may, whether the summons come in the crash of the shattered car, the bowlings of the ocean-storm, the flash of the lightning, or the quiet of our own chamber. We shall feel that the hand of God is in, or over, them all; and when danger threatens, our faculties will rather be quickened than diminished by the consciousness, that, in times of emergency, if we look to him, he will be the more abounding in pouring his grace upon us to supply our need. Calm, self-possessed courage comes to us the moment we lean upon God for strength; while we are rendered helpless by fear, or rash by arrogance, if we look only to ourselves.

There are those who would feel that they were passing away by the will of God, if disease came to them with slowly wasting hand, and would meet his will, coming in that form, with meekness and patience; perhaps, with willingness: and yet were they called to die by sudden casualty, would pass into eternity, shrieking with terror. Much of this fear of sudden death is a mere physical passion, arising from a mistaken idea that there must be great pain in a death by violence; and some even, in spite of the direct teaching of the Lord to the contrary, look upon such a death as a manifestation of the wrath of God against the individual. Yet there is, in fact, much less suffering in most deaths by casualty than by prolonged disease; while in many such there is probably entire freedom from suffering. The mercy of God, no less than his power, is everywhere, and in all forms of death, no less than in life; and were our love for him as universal as his for us, we could no more fear while remembering that we are in his hands, than the infant fears while clasped to its mother's breast.

The possession of this trust in God, because it makes one calm in all positions and under all emergencies, is the surest of all safeguards against danger. How often, in the shocking records of disaster by land and water, is the loss of life directly traceable to the want of that true courage that retains self-possession everywhere, and under all circumstances, giving the power to ward off threatening danger, even when it seems most imminent and irresistible. In pestilence, the terrified are the first to fall victims to the scourge, while none walk so securely as those who possess their souls in quietness.

Intellectual courage,—the courage of thought—comes second in the ascending scale. As physical courage gives us the ability to use our faculties with the same freedom in the most imminent danger as we should with no alarming circumstance to excite us, making us as it were to rise above circumstance, so intellectual courage gives us the power to think with independence, just as we should if we did not know the opinion of another human being upon the subject which engages our thoughts.

Persons having an humble estimate of their own abilities are apt to take their opinions, without reserve, from those whom they most respect, without making any effort on their own part to judge for themselves between truth and falsehood. If this were right, it would take all responsibility in relation to matters of thought from this class of persons; yet every human being must be responsible for the opinions he holds. We cannot excuse ourselves by saying we took our opinion from another, and it is his fault if it be false. Each one must be prepared to answer for his own opinions, just as he must be responsible for his own actions.

Persons of a combative disposition take just the opposite course from this, and adopt opinions merely because they are opposed to some particular person or to some class of persons.

Such persons fancy themselves very independent, and announce their opinions with a movement of the head, that seems to say, "You see I am afraid of nobody, and dare to think for myself." There is, however, quite as little independence in adopting an opinion because somebody else does not think so, as in accepting it because he does. Independence of thought is thinking without any undue regard to the opinion of any one else, one way or the other.

A third class of persons, having large love of approbation, is very numerous. These are unwilling to express any opinion in conversation until they have ascertained the views of the person they address; cannot tell what they think of a book until they know what the critics say; and seem to have no idea of truth in itself, but look merely to please others by changing their opinions as often as they change their companions. There are many authors of this class who, in writing, strive only to please the vanity of the reader by presenting him with a reflection of his own ideas; and whose constant aim is to follow public opinion, instead of leading it. They do not care whether the ideas they promulgate are true or false, if they are but popular; and if they fail to please, are filled with chagrin, and sometimes have even died of despair.

A fourth class of persons, possessed of strong self-esteem, arrive at independence of thought through pride of intellect, and this is even more dangerous than to depend upon others for our opinions; for of all idolatry, there is none so interior and hard to overcome as the worship of self. If we would arrive at truth of opinion, we must be independent of our own passions and prejudices no less than of our neighbor's. There is but one source of truth, and whoever believes that he finds it elsewhere is an idolater. The Lord has declared, "I am the way and the truth and the life"; and it is only through him as the way that we can find the truth, and we seek it through him when we love it because he is the truth, and so seek it for its own absolute beauty and excellence, desiring to bring it out into life.

Look where we may along the pages of history and the records of science, it is the devout men who have been the successful promulgaters of new ideas and searchers after truth. The scoffer and the infidel make great boasts of their progress through their independence of Scripture; but in a little while a devout man follows in their footsteps and proves that their deductions are false, and that even their observations of facts were not to be trusted. Scoffers and infidels come, promising to set the world in order by subverting governments; but though they are quick to pull down, they have no power to build up; and it is only when the devout man comes, that the reign of anarchy and misrule ceases.

Common, daily life is the epitome of history. The devout man is the only one whose opinions are trustworthy; and just so far as we become truly devout will the scales that hinder us from seeing the truth fall from our eyes. "If the eye be single," looking to the Lord alone, unbiassed in its gaze by the thousand-fold passions of earth, "the whole body shall be full of light."

Moral courage, the third phase of this virtue, is that faculty of the soul by which we are enabled to act, in all the social relations of life, with perfect independence of the opinions of the world, and governed only by the laws of abstract propriety, uprightness, and charity. It gives us power to say and to do whatever we conscienciously believe to be right and true, without being influenced by the fear of man's frown or the hope of his favor. This is very difficult, because the customs and conventionalisms of society hedge us about so closely from our very infancy, that they constrain us when we are unconscious of it, and lead us to act and to refrain in a way which our better judgment would forbid, did we consult its indications without being influenced by the world.

It was a saying of a wise man, that "he who fears God can fear nothing else"; and there is certainly no healthy way in which we can be delivered from that fear of the world which destroys moral courage, but the learning to fear, above all things, failing to fulfil our duty before God. If we would have moral courage, we must accustom ourselves to feel that we are accountable to God, and to him only, for what we do. There is a spurious moral as well as intellectual courage, the offspring of pride and arrogance, that pretends to independence in a spirit of defiance of the opinion of the world; but this will never give us the power to act wisely, for wisdom is ever the twin sister of charity that loves the neighbor even while differing from him in opinion. True courage of every kind is perfectly self-possessed, but never defiant. A spirit of defiance springs from envy or hate if it be honest, and from a consciousness of inferiority if assumed; and is sometimes only a disguise self-assumed by fear, when it seeks to be unconscious of itself. True moral courage results from the hope that we are acting in harmony with the laws of eternal wisdom. Fear of every kind is annihilated by a living hope that the Lord is on our side.

If we would test the quality of our moral courage, we must ask ourselves, is it defiant? is it disdainful? is it envious? does it hate its neighbor? or are its emotions affected in any way by the opinion of the world? If we can answer all these questions in the negative, we must go a step farther, and ask if we have gained a state of independence of our own selfish passions, as well as of the world; for our most inveterate foes, and those before whom we cower most abjectly, are often those that dwell within the household of our own hearts. If the love of ease or of sensual indulgence rules there, we need to summon our moral courage to a stern strife, for there is no conquest more difficult than over the evil affections that are rooted in our sensual nature. Wise and good men have gone so far as to believe that this conquest is never entire in this world; that the allurements of indolence and the gnawing of sensual cravings are never quieted save when the body perishes. It is, however, difficult to believe that passions exist in the body apart from the soul, and if not, there can be no absolute impossibility of conquest, even in this world. If this may be attained, it must be through the building up of a true moral courage, that shall fight believing that the sword of the Lord is in the hand of him who strives, trusting in that eternal strength which is mighty even as we are weak.

Religious courage develops naturally in proportion as the growth of moral courage becomes complete. Fear is nowhere so distressing as in our relations with our Creator. That which is by nature best becomes worst when it is perverted; and as the blessed hope to which, as children of God, we are all born heirs, is in its fulness an infinite source of joy and blessing to the soul, so when it is reversed and perverted into fear, it becomes the source of unspeakable misery, sometimes resulting in one of the most wretched forms of insanity.

The morbid state of the mind which induces this distressing passion is the result of a peculiar form of egotism, which leads the thoughts to fasten upon one's own evils so entirely that the mind ceases to recognize, or even to remember, the long-suffering patience and mercy of the Heavenly Father. A more common, but less painful form of this fear is the result of vagueness in one's ideas of the Divine character and attributes. The clear and rational views which Swedenborg has given of the Divine Providence is undoubtedly the reason why religious melancholy is almost never found among the members of the New Church. The peace in believing, which is almost universal among this class of Christians, is a subject of remark among those who observe them, wherever they are found; and this arises, not merely from their not looking upon God as an enemy and avenger who demands a perfect fulfilment of the letter of the law, or infinite punishment for sin, either personally or by an atoning Saviour; but from the possession of a distinct idea, imaged in their minds, of the nature and the quality of the Divine Providence. Where there is a tendency to any kind of fear, nothing increases it more than the want of a distinct idea of the thing or person feared; because the Imagination, which is always quick with the timid, is almost sure to create something within the mind far more fearful than anything that really exists. The greatest boon mankind ever received through a brother man was the doctrine first promulgated by Swedenborg, that God has respect even to our good intentions; and that he casts out none who sincerely desire to be of his kingdom. If one distinctly believes this doctrine, there is no rational ground in the mind for fear; because the very fact of our desire for salvation—provided we understand salvation to be a state of the mind, and not a mere position in a certain place,—or something pertaining to our internal, and not to our external, nature—makes it impossible that we should fail of attaining it.

If one is oppressed with religious fear, the way to escape from it is to use every endeavor to attain a clear and distinct idea of the Divine character, and to strive to bring one's self into harmony with it;—to think as little as possible about one's own sins, and to train the thoughts to dwell upon the Divine perfections, and cultivate an ardent desire to imitate them. It is necessary to think of one's self enough to refrain from the commission of external sins, and just so far and so fast as we put away sin, the Lord will implant the opposite virtue in its place, provided we put the sin away from love to him, and not from any selfish or worldly motive. This state of active cooperation with the Lord is something very different from that into which one falls who is the subject of religious fear, and cannot exist in company with it. The religious coward can only overcome his fear by remembering that God is not a tyrant who demands impossibilities of his slaves, but a Father of infinite love, who would make his children eternally happy; and who, in order that they may become so, gives them every means and every aid that they will receive. He must not suffer his heart to sink within him by thinking of his own weakness, but must elevate it by thinking of the infinite power of him who has called us to salvation. Above all things, he must not fall into reveries about himself, but seek to forget self in the active performance of duty.

The performance of duty, the fulfiling of use, which, rightly understood, is the universal panacea against all the troubles and sorrows of this life, is too often a fearful bugbear in the eyes of those who understand it not. This subject, however, brings us to the third and last topic to be discussed under the head of Life. The love of duty, to be effectual or real, must be earnest; for earnestness is the certain result of living Affection. Through this, all our other powers and faculties ultimate themselves in external Life. Earnestness is the exact opposite of indolence. It is the external motive power, just as Affection is the internal motive power,—the body, of which Affection is the soul. Without earnestness, all our other powers come to naught, and we live in vain; with it, our other endowments become alive, and ready to impress themselves upon the external world. Indolence is a rust, corroding and dulling all our faculties; earnestness, a vitalizing force, quickening and brightening them. By earnestness, alone, can we climb upward in that progress which, begun in time, pauses not at the grave, but passing through the portal of death, goes eternally on in the same direction which we chose for ourselves here, ever approaching more nearly to the Divine perfection, whose life is the unresting activity of infinite love. By indolence, we sink ever lower and lower, and through a continuous process of deterioration, grow each day more unfit for the heavenly life, which all but the abandoned, and perhaps even they, fancy they desire, even when refusing to use any of the means whereby it may be gained.

In the circle of man's evil propensities, no one, perhaps, is a more fruitful mother of wretchedness and crime than the propensity to indolence. It is a common saying, that the love of money is the root of all evil; but that root often runs deeper, and finds its life in indolence, which incites those under its dominion to seek money through unlawful means. The desire for money impels most men to constant effort, and there is no reason for attributing a stronger desire to him who steals or defrauds than to him who labors steadfastly, every day of his life, from early dawn to eve; yet we praise the latter, and condemn the former. It is not, then, the love of money that we condemn, but the desire to attain it by vicious means; and such desire results from a hatred for labor, which is the only legitimate means by which it may be gained. Money in itself is but dead matter, serving only as a minister to some end beyond; and the simple desire for it is neither good nor bad: the end for which it is desired elevates the desire itself to a virtue, or degrades it to a vice; and the means which we adopt for obtaining it, and the purposes to which we apply it, make it either a blessing or a curse.

Every possession, whether moral, intellectual, or physical, is the legitimate reward of labor wisely and earnestly applied; and for these rewards the virtuous are content to labor without repining, and to them, not only the rewards, but the labor itself, is blessed. The vicious, on the contrary, desire the rewards, but hate the labor by which they should be gained. They, therefore, accordingly as they belong to different classes of society, simulate virtues which they do not possess, pretend to acquirements they have been too idle to gain, or strive after wealth by any means, rather than patient industry and honest effort.

It is not the vicious alone who fail to perceive that labor is a blessing from which a wise man can never fly. The curse applied to Adam, "In the sweat of thy face shalt thou eat bread," has led many to suppose that originally the wants of the human race were supplied without any exertion of its own,—that in the garden of Eden there was enjoyment without effort, possession without labor. Even in the pulpit, labor is sometimes spoken of as a curse pertaining only to life in this world, from which we shall be delivered in the life to come. Nothing can be farther from the truth. Employment is the life of every soul, from the Most High down to the least of his children. They only who are spiritually dead, or sleeping, ask for idleness. It is man fallen who looks on labor as a curse, not man walking with God in the garden of Eden; and to man, when he has fallen, labor is indeed a curse, for his soul is so perverted that he knows not the true nature and qualities of a blessing.

Man, resting in thought or feeling, is at best a useless abstraction; he becomes truly a man only when his thoughts and feelings come forth into life, and impress themselves on outward things. If he fail to do this, the rust of idleness eats into all his powers, till he becomes a useless cumberer of the ground; the world loses, and heaven gains nothing when this mortal puts on immortality. Such a being is dead while he lives—a moral paralytic. His capacities are as seed cast upon a rock where there is no earth.

God works incessantly. His eye knows no closing, his hand no weariness. The universe was not only built by his power, but is sustained every moment by his inflowing life. If he were to turn from it for a single instant, all things would return to chaos. Man, created in the image and likeness of God, resembles him most nearly when the life influent from God which fills his soul, flows forth freely as it is given, quickening with its powers all that comes within the influence of his sphere.

There is an old proverb that tells us, "Idleness is the devil's pillow"; and well may it be so esteemed, for no head ever rested long upon it, but the lips of the evil spirit were at its ear, breathing falsehood and temptation. The industrious man is seldom found guilty of a crime; for he has no time to listen to the enticings of the wicked one, and he is content with the enjoyments honest effort affords. It is the vicious idler, vexed to see the fortunes of his industrious neighbor growing while he is lounging and murmuring, who robs and murders that he may get unlawful gain. It is the merry, thoughtless idler who, to relieve the nothingness of his days, seeks the excitement of the wine-cup and the gaming-table. It is the sensual idler, whose licentious ear is open to the voice of the tempter as often as his track crosses the pathway of youth and innocence.

Not only by reason of the external, palpable rewards which labor brings is it to be considered a blessing; but every hour of patient labor, whether with the hands, or in study, or thought, brings with it its own priceless reward, in its direct effects upon the Character. By it the faculties are developed, the powers strengthened, and the whole being brought into a state of order; provided we do all things for the glory of God. "But," exclaims the impatient heart, wearied with the cares of daily life, "how can all this labor for the preservation and comfort of the merely mortal body, this study of things which belong merely to the material world, subserve in any way the glory of God?" It is by these very toils, worthless and transitory as they may seem, that the Character is built up for eternity; and so to build up Character is the whole end for which the things of time were created. No matter how small the duty intrusted to our performance, by performing it to the best of our abilities we are fitting ourselves to be rulers over many things,—to hear the blessed proclamation, "Well done, good and faithful servant; enter thou into the joy of thy Lord."

We are prone, at times, to feel as though we were not placed in the right niche; and that, if we were differently situated, and occupied with employments more worthy our capacities, we should work with pleasure and assiduity; but our present duties are so much beneath us, it seems degrading to spend our time and thoughts upon them. Here is a radical error of judgment, for it is not a high or low duty that degrades or elevates man, but the performing any duty well or ill. It is as true as it is trite, that the honor or shame lies in the mode of performance, not in the quality of the duty. We all, perhaps, know and say, and yet need to be reminded, that a bad president stands lower in the scale of being than a good town officer; a wicked statesman, let him occupy what social position he may, fills a lower place than a conscientious slave who faithfully fulfils the duties of his station.

The first Church, represented by Adam, fell because it ceased to look to the Lord as the source of all life and light, and looked only to itself for all things. It thus lost all conception of the legitimate aim of life. Seeking only the enjoyment of the present moment, labor seemed a dire calamity; for the eternal end of labor, that is, the development of the powers of the soul, so as best to fit it for the performance of heavenly uses, passed out of the knowledge of man, and he learned to look forward to heaven as a place of idle enjoyment; toiling sorrowfully through this world, in the sweat of his face, for bread that, when attained, gave him no true life. To eat bread in the sweat of the face signifies by correspondences, to receive and appropriate as good only that which self may call self-produced and self-owned; and to turn away with aversion from that which is heavenly. This is precisely what we all do when we shrink from, or despise, any labor which duty demands at our hands. The Lord places us in that position in life which is best adapted to overcome the evil dispositions of our nature, and to cultivate our souls for heaven. Perhaps we have capacities that would enable us to perform duties that would be considered by the world of a higher character; but perhaps, on the other hand, we have vices that the Lord is striving to overcome by placing us in this very position which so frets and disgusts us. If we will but remember that the mercy and love of the Lord strive to bless us by fitting us for heaven, and not by making us eminent in the eyes of men, we shall probably find it much easier to comprehend why we are placed as we are in this world. When we torment ourselves by thinking of the inappropriateness of our position in this world, we are always viewing our position with regard to this world only, and therefore all things are dark to us. When we look humbly to the Lord, and seek to find out the eternal ends of his providence in the circumstances of our lives, gradually the scales pass from our eyes, and at last we go in peace, seeing.

Beside the education of our powers and faculties, employment is a blessing in helping us to bear the severest trials of this life. When bereavement or disappointment overwhelms the soul with anguish, so that this world seems only the dark habitation of despair; when we cannot see the bow of promise in the black cloud that darkens our horizon; when we feel that we are without God in the world,—and there are few if any human beings who have not found themselves at some time in such a state,—then, as we hope by the grace of God ever to escape from this despair, we should fly idleness as we would fly the dagger or the poisoned cup; and though grief be tugging at the heart-strings, though our eyes are blinded with tears, we should set ourselves diligently about doing something that may help to make others happy, and let no duty go unperformed; and it will not be long ere the dimmed eyes shall begin to see the glow of the sunshine above, and the earth radiant with beauty below; while, so far from being deserted of God, we shall feel that sorrow has brought us more distinctly than ever before into his presence.

"The path of sorrow, and that path alone,
Leads to the land where sorrow is unknown."

What are the employments of heaven we cannot know with any particularity. Swedenborg tells us that the angels are constantly performing uses; but what these uses are we are not distinctly told. We know that they correspond in some way to the employments of earth; but really to understand them probably transcends our capacities while we remain in the flesh. The conscientious performance of the material and finite uses of this life is the only means by which we can prepare ourselves for the spiritual and eternal uses pertaining to the heavenly kingdom; uses which probably serve to comfort, nourish, and strengthen the soul in eternity, as on earth the corresponding uses serve the wants of the body.

In the spiritual world the spiritual body is fed, clothed, and sheltered in much the same way, to appearance, as is the material body in the natural world; but all the surroundings of the spirit correspond to the state of each individual being, and are the direct gift of the Lord. All the arts and trades of this life do not exist in the other, but as these arts and trades, as well as everything else in this world, exist only through their correspondence with something in the other world, it follows that all the occupations of this life have not similar, but corresponding, occupations in the other. The end of life in this world is to fit the soul for entering upon the heavenly life, and the end of life in heaven is perpetual advancement in spiritual graces and perfections; for no angel, even in the highest heavens, has reached a degree of perfection so high that he can go no further. The end of heavenly life thus being infinite, the effort and employment of that life must be ceaseless. In speaking of ceaseless effort, it must not be understood that this resembles at all the wearying labor of a slave, or that there is anything oppressive or forced about its performance; for this could only be anticipated with dread. Heavenly employment must be full of life and joy, bearing us upward like the wings of a skylark, as he bathes in the sunlight of the upper ether, and carols forth his joy. There will undoubtedly be a variety, too, in heavenly employment, corresponding with our varying states, and making tedium impossible. This may be illustrated by imagining what would be a perfect mode of spending a day in this world. We wake in the morning refreshed by repose, and as we look forth at the sun our spirits rejoice in the beauty of the wakening day, and rise toward the heavenly throne in prayer and praise. We set about the performance of our daily duties, and Christian charity toward those for whose happiness or benefit, whether physical or intellectual, we exert our powers, makes us faithful in whatever we do, that it may be done to the best of our ability; and our effort is lightened by the consciousness of duty done from pure and upright motives. If we go forth for refreshment, communion with nature and the God of nature fills our souls with peace, while the fresh air gives new life to the frame. When the duties of the day are over, and the family circle collects around the evening lamp, reading or conversation awakes the powers of the heart and the intellect, and draws more closely the bonds of the domestic affections. We retire for the night, and ere composing ourselves to sleep, we collect our thoughts, reflect upon the events of the day, examining what we have done well or ill, and prepare by wise resolutions for future effort. We slumber, and the repose of all our powers renews our strength for the coming morrow. Through the whole of this twenty-four hours, employment has been constant. There has been labor of the hands, labor of the head, conversation, thought, prayer, sleep. Every part of the being has been called into exercise; there has been no weariness from labor, and no idleness; but every moment of this whole day has added its quota towards promoting the growth of the whole being; and this is a heavenly day. The more perfectly we can make the occupations of our days thus combine for the growth of our being, the better we are preparing ourselves for the days of heaven.

As the progress of the heavenly life will be infinite, the wants of our spiritual natures must likewise be infinite. The heavenly life must be a life of charity,—a life in which every soul will strive to aid every other to the utmost; and the charities of heaven must strengthen and comfort the soul in a manner corresponding to the aid material charities effect in this world.

Let it constantly be borne in mind, that charities are duties well performed, of whatever kind they may be,—as well the faithful fulfilment of an avocation as the aiding of a suffering fellow-being. Charity is but another name for duty; or rather duty becomes charity when we perform it from genuine love to the Lord and to the neighbor; and whoever leads a life of charity in this world is fitting himself to perform the higher charities that will be required of him in heaven.

The true end and highest reward of labor is spiritual growth; and such growth brings with it the most exalted happiness we are capable of attaining. This happiness is the kingdom of heaven within us; and it is the certain and unfailing reward, or rather consequence, of a life of true charity. It is not difficult, by intellectual thought, to perceive the truth of this doctrine; but this is not enough. We must elevate our hearts into a wisdom that shall make us not only perceive, but feel and love this truth. Until we can do this, we do not truly believe, though we may think we do. If we fret and murmur; if we are impatient and unfaithful; if, when we plainly see that our duty lies in one path, we yet long to follow another; if we know that we cannot leave our present position without dereliction from right, and yet hate or despise the place in which we are; if we repine because God does not give us the earthly rewards we fancy we deserve, though we well know he promises only heavenly ones; if we do habitually any or all of these things, we may know that our faith is of the lip, and not of the heart,—that the life of charity is not yet begun within us. Such repinings, such cravings as these do not belong nor lead to the heavenly kingdom.

He who thinks wisely can never live a life of idleness, and where there is excessive indolence of the body there is never healthy action of the mind. A life of use is a life of holiness; and a life of idleness is a life of sin. He who performs no social use, who makes no human being happier or better, is leading a life of utter selfishness; is walking in a way that ends in spiritual death. In the parable of the sheep and the goats, the King condemns those on the left hand, not because they have done that which was wrong, but because they have omitted doing that which was right.

No human being in possession of his mental faculties is so incompetent that he can do nothing for the benefit of those around him. One prostrate on a bed of sickness might seem, at first glance, incapable of performing any use; and yet, not unfrequently, what high and holy lessons of patient faith, of unwavering piety, are taught by such a being,—lessons that can never die out from the memory of those who minister at the couch of suffering. When the body lies powerless, and the hand has lost its cunning, when even the tongue is palsied in death, how often has the eye, still faithful to the heavenly Master, by a glance of holy peace performed the last act of charity to the bereaved ones whom it looks upon with the eye of flesh for the last time. So long as life remains to us our duties are unfinished: God yet desires our service on earth, and while he desires let us not doubt our capacity to serve. Even for one in the solitude of a prison-cell, when acts of charity become impossible, the duty of labor is not taken away. One may still work for the Father in Heaven, though sitting in darkness, and with manacled limbs. To possess the soul in patience, to be meek, forgiving, and pious, are duties amply sufficient to tax the powers of the strongest. There is no room for idleness even here.

To work is not only a duty, but a necessity of our nature, and when we fancy ourselves idle, we are in fact working for one whose wages is death. The question is never, Shall we work? but, For whom shall we work? Whom shall we choose for our master? and our happiness here and hereafter must depend on the answer we give to this question. We may not deliberately put and deliberately reply to this question in stated words; but our whole lives answer it in one long-continued period. Those who labor steadfastly, with no end in view but the acquisition of worldly, perishable advantages, answer it fearfully; but theirs is not a more desperate reply than comes from the idler and the slothful. Wherever there is activity and force there is hope; for though now flowing in a wrong direction, the stream may yet be diverted into channels that shall lead to eternal life. Where there is no activity, where all the faculties of the soul are sunk in the lethargy of indifference, as well may one hope to find living fountains gushing forth into fertilizing streams amid the sands of the African desert. The man of science tells us that living springs exist beneath these sands, and that artesian wells might bring them to the surface; and so in the inmost nature of man, however degraded he may be, Swedenborg tells us there is a shrine that cannot be defiled, through which heavenly influences may come down into his life, and yet save him, if he will receive them ere he passes from this world; but when sloth has become habitual and confirmed, there is almost as little room for hope that this will ever take place as that artesian tubes will ever make the Saharan desert a region of fertility.

The kingdom of evil is readily attained. We have but to follow the allurements of the passions, and we shall surely find it; we have but to fold our hands, and it will come to us. With the kingdom of eternal life it is not so. That is a prize not easily won. Faithful, untiring effort, looking ever toward eternal ends; a constant scrutiny of motives, that they may be pure and true; an earnest, heartfelt, determined devotion to the heavenly Master, to whose service we have bound ourselves by deliberate choice, can alone make sure for us what we seek. For a long time this may require labor almost painful, but if we persevere, our affections will gradually become at one with our faith, the heavenly life will become habitual, so as to be almost instinctive; and when the celestial kingdom is thus established within us, no place will be left for weariness, or doubt, or pain, or fear.

CONVERSATION.

"He who sedulously attends, pointedly asks, calmly speaks, coolly answers, and ceases when he has no more to say, is in possession of some of the best requisites of man."

—LAVATER.

"The common fluency of speech, in many men, and most women, is owing to a scarcity of matter and a scarcity of words; for whoever is master of a language, and has a mind full of ideas, will be apt, in speaking, to hesitate upon the choice of both; whereas, common speakers have only one set of ideas, and one set of words to clothe them in; and these are always ready at the mouth; so people can come faster out of a church when it is almost empty, than when a crowd is at the door."

—SWIFT.

* * * * *

Of all the physical powers possessed by man, there is none so noble as that of speech; none that distinguishes him so entirely from the brute; yet how few there are who seem in any adequate degree to comprehend its power and value, or who ever pause to reflect upon the sacrilegious abuse to which it is often degraded.

Language is Thought and Affection in form, as works are Thought and Affection in life. By language we receive the word of Divine Revelation, and by language we approach the Divine Author of all things in prayer. By language we are made happy in social life, through interchange of thought and feeling with our fellow-beings. By language, man is made lord of the terrestrial world. By language, the wisdom of past ages becomes an inheritance for the whole earth, instead of perishing with each possessor; and thus man advances from age to age, through the experience of the past, instead of being obliged to work out all the wisdom he gains by his own individual effort.

This is the bright and beautiful side of language; but on the other hand is a dark and hideous side, when language becomes the foul and poisonous medium through which the folly, the vice, and all the moral deformities of humanity, are spread abroad through the world, and handed down through the ages. The same medium that serves as a vehicle for heavenly truth is the tool of the scoffing infidel; it is formed into prayer by the saint, and into blasphemy by the sinner. Alternately, it serves the purest and holiest uses, or the vilest and most atrocious abuses; now formed to the sweet breathings of heavenly charity, and anon to the harsh utterances of malignant hate.

These distinctions are wide and clear, and easily perceived by the most obtuse or indifferent observer; but these distinctly marked varieties pass into milder shades as they are exhibited in common Conversation, and then a nicer observation is needful to detect the varieties of hue that color language when used in the every-day forms of society.

The habitual use we make of language is the result of our own characters, and it reacts upon them. It likewise acts upon those who are about us with an unceasing power, repelling or attracting all whom we approach. Every human being exerts a perpetual influence on every other human being, with an activity as universal as that of gravity in the material world; and language is one of the most efficient means of this influence. Viewed in the light of these truths, common Conversation becomes an object of serious consideration; and the mode of sustaining it worthy of the deepest thought and of the most careful watchfulness.

Between the malignity of a fiend and the charity of an angel there is a long interval of inclined plane, and those who walk there may seem a company so mixed that they cannot be separated into two distinct bands; but every individual of the throng is looking toward one or the other extremity, and either ascending or descending in his course. Conversation is the outbirth of our thoughts and affections, and it shows their quality in the most direct manner possible. Actions are said to speak louder than words, and to the appreciation of our fellow-beings our lives are much truer and fuller expositions of our internal natures than our Conversation; but before God, always, and before our own consciences if we really look at ourselves, the insincere words that deceive our fellow-beings stand unmasked,— the deformed exponents of the falsehood of the soul. We can therefore understand the character of our neighbor better by his actions than by his words; but to understand our neighbor is of little importance compared with understanding ourselves; and is chiefly useful because a comparison of individuals aids us in comprehending our own natures. We can understand ourselves by our own words if we will take the trouble to consider them dispassionately, and analyze the thoughts and affections whence they spring.

So little honesty is believed to exist in ordinary Conversation, that the saying of a witty courtier, that "language is the instrument whereby man conceals his thoughts," has almost passed into a proverb. The question, in which direction is the man walking who wraps duplicity about himself as his constant garment, needs no answer; for all must know that the Divine Being, whose form is truth, hateth a lie.

The first element in Conversation should be sincerity. Not the blunt and harsh sincerity sometimes met with, which is made the cloak of self-esteem and bitterness; for that is an evil of the same nature as the malice and hatred that show themselves in active, outward injury towards the neighbor. When excited by pride or anger, the tongue needs a bridle no less than the hand; and when the heart can utter itself truly only in the forms of such passions, silence is its only safeguard. In speaking of the follies or vices of others, sincerity should be tempered by a Christian charity, which, while it does not gloss over vice, does not dwell upon it needlessly, nor take a malicious pleasure in spreading it abroad, nor indulge self-complacency by dilating upon it, to give the idea that one is superior to such things.

If such motives are allowed to have sway, a person soon becomes confirmed in the habit of gossiping,—a habit that degrades alike the intellect and the heart. The soul of gossip is a contemptible vanity that imagines itself, or at least would have others imagine it, superior to all that it finds of evil and absurdity in the characters of those whom it passes in review. A very little observation will serve to show any one that everybody sees his neighbors' faults, while very few open their eyes upon their own; and that not unfrequently a person condemns with the utmost vehemence in others precisely the same follies and vices in which he himself habitually indulges. Those who study their own characters with most care, and who best understand themselves, are apt to say least of the characters of their neighbors; they find too much to do within themselves, in curing their own defects, to have time or inclination to sit in judgment upon the defects of others.

It is impossible to indulge habitually in this vice without weakening the powers of the intellect. The heart never suffers alone from the indulgence of any wrong passion. The intellect and the affections ever sink as well as rise together. Where the love of gossip becomes a confirmed habit, the mind loses its power of accurately appreciating the value of Character,—of distinguishing truly between the good and the bad. The power of discrimination is weakened and impaired, so that no confidence can be placed in the opinions of the mind in relation to Character or Life. In addition to this, we must bear in mind that all the mental power we bestow in criticizing and ridiculing our fellow-beings is just so much taken from our mental strength, which we might have applied to some useful intellectual exercise. The strength of the mind is no more indefinite than that of the body. We have but a certain limited amount; and all that we apply to idle or bad purposes is just so much abstracted from the good and the useful.

Sarcasm is a weapon we are almost sure to find constantly used by the gossip; and whether it be shown in the coarse ridicule of the vulgar, or the keen satire of the refined, it springs ever from the same source, and is directed to the same end; as surely as the clumsy war-club of savage lands was invented from the same impulse and wrought with the same intent as the graceful blade of

Damascus. Its source is vanity, its end to make self seem great by making others seem little. It is a weapon that, however skilfully wielded, always cuts both ways, wounding far more deeply the hand that grasps it than the victim it strikes. Of all the powers of wit, sarcasm is the lowest. There is nothing easier than ridicule; nothing requiring a weaker head, or a colder heart.

The sincere lover of truth will never be found habitually indulging either in gossip or sarcasm; for those who are addicted to these vices never tell a story simply as they heard it, never relate a fact simply as it happened. A little is added here or left out there to give the story a more entertaining turn or the satire a keener point. As the habit grows stronger, invention becomes more ready and copious, till at length truth is covered up and lost under an accumulation of fiction.

There is a very common form of insincerity used by a class of well-meaning but injudicious persons, who, rather than wound the feelings of their friends, conceal the truth from them, sometimes by prevarication and sometimes by positive falsehood; doing wrong, that, as they imagine, good may come of it; as though an evil tree could by any possibility bear good fruit.

Another class of persons converse as though the chief sin of Conversation were the wounding the self-love of those to whom they speak, by expressing any difference of opinion from them. Thus they are continually temporizing, and often contradicting themselves, and exhibiting a cowardly meanness of spirit, which is one of the most contemptible of all the varied forms of duplicity.

There is a common form of embarrassment resulting in a hesitation of speech, which often springs from a want of genuine sincerity. The speaker is fancying what others will think of his remarks, instead of fixing his mind entirely on the subject of discourse. In this divided state, his mind loses half its power, and he utters himself in a manner satisfactory neither to himself nor to his hearers. No doubt hesitation in speech sometimes arises from want of verbal skill; but probably a very large proportion of persons suffering from this difficulty would soon cure themselves if they would steadfastly speak what they believe to be truth, just as it rises in their minds, and without stopping to think what will be thought of their opinions or words by those who listen to them.

Next after truth, reverence is perhaps most important if we would order our Conversation aright. Many indulge in a frivolous mode of speech in speaking of the most sacred subjects; which, though it may spring from nothing worse than thoughtlessness, cannot fail to exert a baneful influence on the Character, and diminish, perhaps destroy, the little respect for things holy still cleaving to the heart. This same irreverence shows itself in another form, in speaking of the calamities suffered by others, turning that into a jest which is to those under discussion cause of the most bitter anguish; and though the speakers probably would not for any consideration have their words come to the ears of those spoken of, they still do not hesitate to make food for mirth out of death or sin, poverty or misfortune, in a way little short of inhuman. The indulgence of this habit falls back upon the soul of the perpetrator, wounding deeply, if it does not kill, all the finer sensibilities of the nature; drying up the fountains of sympathy, and making the heart hard and callous.

Akin to reverence, and probably springing from it, is purity; which shows itself by a careful avoidance of everything profane, obscene, coarse, or in any way offending delicacy, either in word, tone, or suggestion. This purity cannot be too much insisted upon; for its opposite poisons the fountains of the heart, defiling the temple which should be a dwelling-place for the Holy Spirit. Delicacy and refinement are too often looked upon merely as the elegant ornaments of polished life. They should, on the contrary, be esteemed essentials in the Christian Character; Everything leaning towards profanity, obscenity, or indelicacy is utterly incompatible with Christian purity of heart. Low attempts at wit, that hinge on vulgarity, are a common form of this vice; and those who indulge their propensities in this direction, are laying the foundation for general grossness of Character, such as they would now, perhaps, shrink from with horror; but towards which they are none the less surely tending.

We are told, that "for every idle word we speak we shall give an account at the day of judgment; for by our words we shall be justified, and by our words we shall be condemned." This has seemed to many a very hard saying, and while some persons try to explain it away, others turn from it as too hard either to explain or to receive. When, however, we reflect on what words really are, we perceive that this heavy accountability clings to them of necessity, as effect to cause. Man was created the image and likeness of God, and when we find points hard of comprehension in the character or relations of man, we may often gain much light by taking a corresponding view, so far as our finite powers permit, of the Divine Being.

The Scriptures are the Divine Word; that is, the verbal exponent of the Divine Mind; while the world around us is the material exponent of the same Mind. Speech and life in humanity correspond to these two modes of expression of the Divinity. When imperfectly understood, they almost of necessity seem to contradict each other; but it is only then. The unity of the Word and Works of God is becoming constantly more apparent as man advances in the knowledge of both. Each helps to explain the other, and it is only by a knowledge of both that the character and attributes of God can be justly comprehended. A little consideration will show that the speech and life of man in like manner combine to exhibit the character and qualities of the soul within,—that they harmonize with each other, and that therefore of necessity by our words no less than by our works we must be justified or condemned before the All-seeing One.

Many suppose, that because we, in our short-sighted views, are so often misled by the words of our fellow-beings, they are not true pictures of Character. We should, however, remember that it is not before short-sighted man that we are to be judged by our words, but before the omniscient God. To his ear our words have a very different significance from that which they bear to our fellow-beings. We should recollect, that the falsehood which may make it impossible for us to judge righteous judgment of our fellow-beings stands before the Lord only as a falsehood; and

117

that, in whatever form it comes, from the courteous white lie—as man dares to call it—of polished society, to the double-dyed blackness of malignant hypocrisy, God sees only the varying shades of dissimulation; springing, in whatever form, from a deep-running undercurrent of selfishness and worldliness. We may be deceived into believing words are genuine when they are not so; but every disingenuous word uttered is, before God, the image and likeness of the duplicity that reigns within. To us they may seem the beautiful garments that envelop purity and truth; but to him they are the foul and flimsy veils that strive to conceal the soul's deformity.

Man, in the pride of his artifice, often exults because he has outwitted his neighbor by his lying words, while all the time he has far more outwitted himself. He has degraded his own soul,— set upon it a foul mark that can be washed out only by the bitter tears of penitence, and yet holds his head aloft in fancied superiority over his fellows, while before God and the angels he stands like Cain, with the mark of sin impressed upon his forehead.

That man should be condemned for lying words all will admit, but when men converse idly, or without any particular thought one way or the other as to what they are saying, they are apt to suppose that no especial moral character belongs to the words they utter. Such, however, is far from the truth. Man is never so sincere as in his idle moments. His words are then the simple outporings of his affections. It has been often said, that one can always measure the refinement of any person by watching his language and deportment in his moments of sportiveness. It is quite as easy to judge of other traits of Character when the mind is thrown off its guard at such moments. Idle words, more apparently than any other, are genuine manifestations of Character. It is in them that the heart, out of its abundance, speaketh. The Conversation of a true Christian is characterized in his hours of gayety, no less than at other times, by truth tempered with love, made clear and steadfast by simplicity, and clothed with reverence and purity.

The trait of Conversation we would next consider is courtesy,—Christian courtesy. This is nothing more nor less than carrying out the law of charity; the doing as we would be done by. It is to recognize the fact that others have a right to talk as well as ourselves; and also a right to expect us to listen to what they say as attentively and respectfully as we would wish them to listen to us. We should not merely hold our tongues when others speak, but should scrupulously attend to what they say. A person who affects politeness, although he remains silent while another speaks, yet does so with an air that plainly shows he is paying no attention to what is said, and is waiting with impatience for the moment when he can hear himself talk. This sort of listening is a mere pretence put on by the conceited and overbearing when they wish to pass for persons of polite manners; but in reality it is an insult rather than a courtesy to listen in this way. To listen with true courtesy, one should feel and show, not only a willingness, but a desire to know what another has to say, should follow attentively all that he says, and should then reply with due consideration for what has been said.

It is a remark often made, that after an argument between two or more persons, each individual is more strongly fixed in his previous opinion than he was before. This result is often consequent upon the want of true courtesy. The parties to an argument, absorbed in admiration of their own opinions, seek not to become wiser through discourse, which should be the end sought in all Conversation of an argumentative or discussive character, but seek only to draw attention to their own views and opinions; until that which should be Conversation degenerates into a mere war of words, in which each party strives to talk down, rather than to convince, the other. In such wordy warfare charity has no part; but pride and combativeness hold entire dominion over the soul. He who comes off conqueror may exult in his own power; but he has overcome, not because reason was on his side, but because his combativeness was stronger than that of his opponent; and he exults in that which is in reality his shame. The moral and the intellectual natures suffer together in

119

such contests. The mind fastens itself upon the prejudices and opinions it has chanced to adopt, loving them merely because they are its own, and seeks no longer to advance in the acquisition of truth; while the heart, inflated with egotism, has no abiding-place for charity. Let charity rule in a discussion, and how different is the result. Each party then strives to aid the other in discovering the truth, and at the close of the Conversation each has made some advance in the knowledge of truth. The ideas of both have become more clear and rational, and their minds have acted with far more power, because they have been given exclusively to the object under consideration instead of being divided between the object and self-love. In the one case, the parties are like two horses harnessed together contrariwise, and each striving to go forward by pulling the other back; while in the other, they travel amicably and fleetly, side by side, toward the fountain of truth.

Next after courtesy comes simplicity, which may be defined as forgetfulness of self. There is nothing more fatal to agreeable Conversation than thinking perpetually of one's self. Young persons, on first going into society, are very apt to fall into the error of supposing that all eyes and ears are fixed upon them, to observe how awkwardly or how gracefully they move, and how well or how ill they converse. This is the result of a mental egotism combined with love of admiration, and usually produces awkward diffidence or absurd affectation. Too often the first weakness is overcome, or covered up, most unwisely, by exchanging bashfulness for impertinent boldness; while the vanity and self-consciousness of the second very rarely result in manners or Conversation either sensible or agreeable. To overcome these defects, wisely, requires a strong effort. They should be radically subdued by learning to ask one's self, "Am I doing what is right and proper?" instead of, "What will people think of me?" It is no easy task to learn to do this habitually, because there is involved in it a radical change of Character. It is to learn to *be*, instead of to *seem*. In the first state, we are absorbed by the idea of what we *seem* to others; while, in the second state, we are occupied with the idea of what we really *are*, without regard to the opinion of anybody, but guided strictly by the abstract law of right. In the first state, we are embarrassed by the complexity of our wishes and aims. We wish to please everybody, and we strive to ascertain what will be agreeable to the various tastes of those with whom we converse. Thus we have no constant landmark, no unvarying compass to guide us on our way; and we are drawn hither and thither, as we try now to please one person and then another. Let our wishes and aims but become simple, and we walk steadily and surely in the light. In the complexity of our desires we were slaves; but in their simplicity we become free. Complexity strives perpetually after reputation, and is always advancing either in the direction of servility or of arrogance, according as self-esteem or the love of admiration predominate in the mind of the individual; and advancing years find it ever deteriorating in all the best elements of Character. Simplicity, on the contrary, deals with what is, and not with what seems to be, and is ever seeking growth in goodness and truth; and therefore each added year finds it growing in all the graces of improving manhood or womanhood. Complexity grows old in mind no less than in body. Its moral being is scarred and wrinkled by selfishness and worldliness, and its intellect dried up and withered by narrow views and unworthy aims. In its old age there is nothing genial or lovely, and in its death one could almost believe that soul as well as body perishes. Simplicity improves in mind as it grows old in body. There are no wrinkles on the brow of its sunny spirit; there is no withering of its intellect. Its life, in time, is a perpetual advance in all that is gracious and intelligent,—a steady ripening for eternity,—and its death is but a birth into a fuller and more perfect life.

In Conversation, complexity adapts itself artfully to others, in order to gratify its own selfishness. It humors the selfishness and whims of those to whom it speaks, in order to gain consideration from them, or to make use of them in some way for its own advancement.

Simplicity, on the contrary, adapts itself artlessly to others, because it is full of charity; and therefore desires to make others

121

happy. Its words are the overflow of genial thought and kindly affection; and all hearts that hold aught in common with it open and expand before its influences as plants start at the touch of spring. It is not so much the words uttered that produce this effect, as the pleasant and kindly way in which they are said; for this throws a grace and an attractive charm about the most commonplace objects of its Conversation.

Intellectual brilliancy in Conversation dazzles and delights the imagination; but it does not touch the heart. Simplicity, on the contrary, always impresses itself upon our feelings with a power that is all the more strong because we cannot analyze it by our intellect. We talk with a person of simplicity about the common occurrences of the day, and find ourselves, we know not why, more gentle, refined, and happy than we were before. We are refreshed as by drinking from a pure and undefiled fountain of sweet waters; refreshed as mere intellectual power cannot refresh us; refreshed as no book can refresh us. There is a harmonious completeness in the whole being of simplicity, a directness and honesty in all it says and does, "a grace beyond the reach of art," in all its manifestations more potent, because more internal in its effects, than anything can ever be that is born merely of the intellect. There is no affectation, no straining for effect in simplicity. All is natural and genuine with it. Its wit is never forced, its wisdom is never stilted; nor is either ever dragged in for mere display. With the simple, Conversation is like a brook flowing through a beautiful country, and reflecting the varied scenes through which it passes in all their grace and beauty.

Another important trait in Conversation is the correct use of words; and the effort after this cannot fail to exert a beneficial influence on the mental powers. In order to speak correctly, one must observe with accuracy and think with justness; the endeavor to do this increases our love for the truth and our capacity for perceiving it. Much of the falsehood in the world is the result of carelessness in observation or phraseology. We often hear two persons give an account of something they have seen or heard, and are surprised at the discrepancies between the two narrations.

Probably neither person intended to deceive; but both saw or heard carelessly, and so are incompetent to describe accurately; and probably, also, neither has cultivated the habit of speaking correctly, as that habit is not apt to be found united with carelessness of observation. Such persons would, perhaps, look upon this sort of carelessness as a venial offence; but it is not so. Anything that interferes with, or diminishes the capacity for, perceiving or speaking the truth is of importance, and should never be passed over lightly. God is truth no less than love, and every variation from the truth is a sin against him.

If we find we have related any fact or described any object incorrectly, it is not enough that we apologize for the error by saying "we though it was so." Such an error should impress us as a thing to be repented of, and we should try to ascertain why and how it was that we fell into it, and it should put us on our guard; that we may be more accurate in future.

Inaccuracy of speech often arises from a desire to tell a good story, resulting from the love of admiration or from an ill-trained imagination. The speaker colors, exaggerates, and distorts everything he relates, carefully conceals all the facts on one side of a question, and enlarges upon those of the opposite side with compensating fulness. It is no uncommon thing to see this carried to such an extent that it is idle to give credence to anything the person says; the more especially as such a person very rarely stops with mere distortion of the facts of a story. As the habit increases, invention supplies new facts and details to make out all the parts desired, till the listener finds it impossible to separate the true from the false, and the speaker is as unable to distinguish his own inventions from the original facts; for when the habit of speaking the truth is neglected, the capacity for perceiving it is gradually lost.

In an intellectual point of view, the correct use of words is of the utmost importance, if one would speak well. To attain this, it is necessary to have a distinct idea of the meaning of words, and then to endeavor to use such words as truly express the ideas of the mind. The use of pet phrases and words is entirely at war with correctness in this respect. With some persons, everything is pretty, from Niagara Falls to the last new ribbon; while others find, or rather make, everything nice, splendid, or glorious. It would be esteemed an insult to the understanding of any person to suppose that the same idea or emotion could be aroused in his mind by the sight of the sublimest work of nature as by a trifling article of dress; yet if he use the same term to describe it in each instance, he certainly lays himself open to such an imputation. Want of thorough education is an inadequate excuse for follies of this sort, because common sense combined with far less knowledge than may be acquired in a common school is more than sufficient to enable every one to use his native tongue with sufficient propriety to save him from being ridiculous.

There is one specious gift which is almost sure to mislead those who are largely endowed with it, and that is fluency. We listen with pain to one who speaks hesitatingly and with difficulty, and who is obliged to search his memory for words that will correctly represent his thoughts; but if, when the words come, we find they really tells us something worth waiting for, we feel far less weariness than in following the unhesitating flow of words that are but empty sound. There is always peculiar ease and pleasure in the exercise of a natural talent, and those naturally possessed of fluency must of course find it hard to restrain the tide of words that is perpetually flowing up to the lips; but if they desire to converse agreeably, the effort must be made, and self-denial must be attained. The benefit derived by an over-fluent talker from self-restraint will be quite commensurate with the effort, no less than with the added pleasure of the listener, for he will gain in the power of accurate thought every time that he resists the inclination to utter an unmeaning sentence.

A clear and distinct utterance is another faculty that should be cultivated, for the effect of an otherwise interesting conversation may be seriously impaired, and perhaps destroyed, by a slovenly or indistinct articulation. Every word and syllable should receive its due quantity of sound, yet without drawling or stiffness; while the voice should be so modulated as to be heard without effort, and yet the opposite fault of speaking too loud is avoided.

Correct pronunciation is a very desirable accomplishment, though somewhat difficult to attain in its details, authorities are so various; but probably the most comprehensive rule that can be observed is, as far as possible to avoid provincialisms. A person's pronounciation can hardly be elegant if it reveal at once of what State or city he is a native; while freedom from local peculiarities is of itself a promise of good pronunciation, as it shows either that the individual has taken pains to weed out such peculiarities, or that he has been bred among those who have done so. The pronunciation of the best scholars in every part of our country is very similar, while the difference becomes more and more strongly marked between the inhabitants of the various States of the Union as we descend in the scale of education.

Finally, do not fear to be silent when you have nothing to say. Do not talk for the mere sake of talking. To sit silently and abstractedly, as if one were among but not of the company in which one may chance to be, is discourteous; because it implies a fancied superiority, or an unkind indifference. Good manners require that in company one should be alive to what is going on, but this does not imply the necessity of always talking. There is, almost always, in a mixed company, some Conversation to which a third person may listen without intrusion; but if this should not happen to be the case, it is far better to wait until something occurs that gives one an opportunity of talking to some rational purpose, than to insist that one's tongue shall incessantly utter articulate sounds whether the brain give it anything to say or no. This sort of purposeless talking exerts a positively injurious influence upon the mind, by leading it into the too common error of mistaking sound for sense, words for ideas.

Before quitting this important subject, there is a general view to be taken of it in its universal bearings upon Character, which places it among the most important branches of a wise education.

The true signification of education, according to one derivation of the word, is the bringing or leading out of the faculties. The best educated person is not he who has stored up in his memory the greatest number of facts, but he whose faculties have become most strengthened and perfected by what he has learned.

There are several studies pursued in our schools and colleges, such as Greek, Latin, and Mathematics, rather because they are looked upon as a kind of gymnastics, whereby the mental faculties in general are educated, or developed and invigorated, than because they bring a direct practical benefit to life; for of the numbers who exercise their faculties upon them, while in the schools, not one in ten makes any direct use of them afterwards. These studies require expensive books and teachers, and a greater amount of time than can be given by the majority of men and women; and moreover they cultivate the intellect without doing anything for the heart. Without in any degree questioning or undervaluing the great and varied benefit derived to the mind from these studies in added accuracy, strength, and richness, there is still room for wonder that Conversation, both as a science and an art, has no place in our systems of education; since its practice is a daily necessity to all, while its power, when wielded with skill, is second to none other that is brought to bear upon the social circle.

Our young girls are nearly all of them taught music with great expenditure of money, time, and labor; but whether we look to the cultivation of actual talent, to the improvement of Character, or to accomplishment as a means of making ourselves agreeable in society, how profitably could a part of this time and labor be employed in acquiring the power and the habit of accurate language, agreeable modulation, distinct utterance, and courteous attention; and it can hardly be doubted that a person who possesses the power of conversing well finds and gives more pleasure in society than a person skilled to an equal degree in music.

Conversation has, indeed, this advantage over all school studies; in order to obtain its best requisites no books are needed beyond such as are accessible to all, while its best teachers are the suggestions of common sense, and the conscientious love of the true and the good. Still, there are few persons whose efforts would not be crowned with a higher success if aided by the criticism and the guidance of a competent instructor. Those who are competent to self-instruction in this, as in all other accomplishments, are exceptional examples, and it may be doubted if even these might not have reached a higher excellence, aided by the suggestions of another mind. Properly cultivated, Conversation would have an influence in developing the whole being, of a kind and degree that could hardly be over-estimated. In its exercise, Thought and Affection have full play, while all the stores of Memory and the wealth of Imagination find ample field for display.

Conversation is so comprehensive in its manifestations and necessities, that it can reach its perfection only through the development of the whole being, moral as well as intellectual; and it will constantly become more finished in proportion as this development becomes more complete. Its universality, its hourly necessity, should impress us with its value; for the mercy of the Lord, as it gives light and air, sunshine and shower, seedtime and harvest, in short, all the essentials of physical development to the whole human race, so it supplies to all the power and the essential means for disciplining and cultivating the whole Character.

MANNERS

"There is something higher in Politeness than Christian moralists have recognized. In its best forms, as a simple, out-going, all-pervading spirit, none but the truly religious man can show it; for it is the sacrifice of self in the little habitual matters of life,—always the best test of our principles,—together with a respect, unaffected, for man, as our brother under the same grand destiny."

—C. L. BRACK.

"Manners are what vex or soothe, corrupt or purify, exalt or debase, barbarize or refine us, by a constant, steady, uniform, insensible operation, like that of the air we breathe in."

—BURKE.

* * * * *

Manners are the most external manifestation by which men display their individual peculiarities of mind and heart; and unless used artificially to conceal the true Character, they form a transparent medium through which it is exhibited.

It has been sarcastically asserted, that few persons exist who can afford to be natural; and it is probable that if the human race were to allow their manners to be perfectly natural; that is, were they to allow all the passions of the soul to display themselves without restraint in their manners, social intercourse would become insupportable. Among the merely worldly, the difference between an ill-bred and a well-bred person is that the former displays his discomfort, ill-humor, or selfishness in his Manners, while the latter conceals them all under a veil of suavity and kindness. Selfishness prompts the one to be rude, and the other to be hypocritical, and each is alike unworthy of commendation.

Manners are the garments of the spirit; the external clothing of the being, in which Character ultimates itself. If the Character be simple and sincere, the Manners will be at one with it; will be the natural outbirth of its traits and peculiarities. If it be complex and self-seeking, the Manners will be artificial, affected, or insincere. Some persons make up, put on, take off, alter, or patch their Manners to suit times and seasons, with as much facility, and as little apparent consciousness of duplicity, as if they were treating their clothes in like fashion. If an individual of this class is going to meet company with whom he wishes to ingratiate himself, he puts on his most polished Manners, as a matter of course, just as he puts on his best clothes; and when he goes home, he puts them off again for the next important occasion. For home use, or for associating with those about whose opinion he is indifferent, no matter how rude the Manners, or how uncared for the costume. Perhaps the rudeness may chance to come out in some overt act that will not bear passing over in silence, and then the perpetrator utters an "excuse me," that reminds one of a bright new patch set upon an old faded garment. Not that such a patch is unworthy of respect when worn by honest poverty, and set on with a neatness that makes it almost ornamental. This is like the "excuse me" of a truly, well-bred man, apologizing for an offence he regrets; while the "excuse me" of the habitually rude man is like the botched patch of the sloven or the beggar, who wears it because the laws of the land forbid nakedness.

The fine lady of this class may be polished to the last degree, when arrayed in silks and laces she glides over the rich carpets of the drawing-room; and yet, with her servants at home, she is possibly less the lady than they; or worse still, this fine lady, married, perhaps, to a fine gentleman of a character similar to her own, in the privacy of domestic life carries on a civil war with him, in which all restraint of courtesy is set aside.

There is so much undeniable hypocrisy in the high-bred courtesy of polished society, that among many religious persons there has come to be an indifference, nay, almost an opposition, to Manners that savor of elegance or courtliness. If, however, Christian charity reign within, rudeness or indifference cannot reign without. One may as well look for a healthy physical frame under a skin revolting from disease, as for a healthy moral frame under Manners rude and discourteous; for Manners indicate the moral temperament quite as accurately as the physical temperament is revealed by the complexion. Selfishness and arrogance of disposition express themselves in indifferent, rude, or overbearing Manners; while vanity and insincerity are outwardly fawning and sycophantic. If Christian charity reign in the heart, it can fitly express itself only in Manners of refinement and courtesy; and the Christian should not be unwilling to wear such Manners in all sincerity, because the worlding assumes them to serve his purposes of selfishness. Worldly wisdom ever pays Virtue the compliment of imitation; but that is no good reason why Virtue should hesitate to appear like herself. The best Manners possible are the simple bringing down of the perfect law of charity into the most external ultimates of social life. Until Character tends at all times, and in all places, and towards all persons, to ultimate itself in Manners of thorough courtesy, it is not building itself upon a sure foundation. The ultimates of all things serve as their basis and continent; therefore must true charity of heart be built upon and contained within true charity of Manner.

When we are in doubt regarding the value of any particular trait of Character, we can generally find the solution of our difficulty by working out an answer to the question, How does it affect our usefulness in society? There are three modes in which we express ourselves towards those with whom we come in contact in the family and social relations of life,—Action, Conversation, and Manners. The importance of ordering the first two of these expressions aright can hardly be doubted by any thinking being; but that conscience has anything to do with Manners would probably be questioned by many. Let us ascertain the moral bearing of Manners by the test just indicated.

What effect have our Manners upon our usefulness as social beings? Conversation is in general the expression of our thoughts; much more seldom do we express our affections in words. Manners, on the contrary, are the direct expression of our affections. They are to Action what tone is to Conversation. Many persons may be found who make use of falsehood in their Conversation, but very few who can lie in the tones of their voice. So many persons can act hypocritically, but there are comparatively few whose Manners are habitually deceitful. Our words and actions are more easily under our control than our tones and manners; because the former are more the result of Thought, while the latter are almost entirely the result of Affection. Although few persons are distinctly aware of this difference, every one is powerfully affected by it. There is no physical quality more powerful to attract or to repel than the tones of the voice; and this power is all the stronger because both parties are usually unconscious of it; and so mutually act and are acted upon, simply and naturally, without effort or resistance. Thus conversation often owes its effect less to the words used than to the tones in which they are uttered. An unpalatable truth may come without exciting any feeling of irritation or opposition from one who speaks with a tone of voice expressive of the benevolent affections, and produce much good; while the very same words, uttered in a tone of asperity or bitterness, may exasperate the hearer, and be productive only of harm. It has already been said, that Manners bear the same relation to life that tone bears to conversation; and a good life loses great portion of the power it might exert over those who come within the influence of its sphere if it ultimate itself in ungracious or repulsive Manners. In the old English writers we often find persons characterized as Christian gentlemen or Christian ladies; and courtesy seems formerly to have been clearly understood to be a Christian virtue. Our conflict with, and our escape from, the aristocracy and privileges of rank of older nations has caused a reaction, not only against them, but also against the external politeness which was connected with them, and which was, and is too often, though certainly not always, false and hypocritical; and thus the growth of republican principles has had the effect to diminish the respect once entertained for good Manners, and the mass of our countrymen seem to look upon politeness as an antiquated remnant of a past age, which the present has outgrown as entirely as wigs and hoop-petticoats. It is, however, a curious feature in the change, that at no previous time have the titles of gentleman and lady been so universally and pertinaciously assumed as at the present. The rudest even are resentful at being called simply men or women, while they unconsciously show the weakness of their claim to a higher title by denying it to those who they assume are no better than themselves. The often-repeated anecdote of the Yankee stage-driver who asked of the Duke of Saxe Weimer, "Are you the man that wants an extra coach?" and on being answered in the affirmative, said, "Then I am the gentleman to drive you," is an illustration of what is going on continually around us. A large proportion of the members of one half of society stands in perpetual fear that those in the other half do not esteem them gentlemen and ladies; and yet it seldom seems to occur to them to substantiate their claim to the coveted title by that cultivation of good Manners, which can alone make it theirs of right.

The artificial Manners and laws of social life are so overloaded with conventionalisms, and a knowledge of these is so often made a test of good-breeding, that much confusion of opinion exists regarding the requisites that constitute the true gentleman and lady. These titles belong to something real, something not dependent on the knowledge and practice of conventionalisms that change with every changing season, but to substantial qualities of Character which are the same yesterday, to-day, and to-morrow.

The foundation of good Manners is the sincere acknowledgment that we are all children of one great family, all one band of brothers, each having a right to receive from the rest all the consideration and forbearance that can be given him without diminishing the portion that belongs to the others. The rich complain of the envy and jealousy of the poor, and the poor murmur because of the arrogance and haughtiness of the rich; yet if those among the two classes who are guilty of these vices were to change positions, they would change vices too; for arrogance *in* the possessor and envy *towards* the possessor of wealth are but differing phases of a love for wealth based on the love for that consideration in society which it gives, and not for the power it yields of added usefulness.

The ill-bred fashionist sails haughtily into the shop where she obtains materials for her adornment, and with a supercilious air purchases her ribbons and laces of a sulky girl, who revenges herself for not being able to wear the costly gauds by treating as rudely as she dares the customer who can; and as they look upon each other, the one with scorn, and the other with envious hate, we see in both only the very same littleness of feminine vanity, which in its narrow-minded silliness believes that the first requisite of a lady is costly garments.

It would be a great mistake to suppose that in our higher society there are no good Manners, none that are really good in essence and purpose, as well as in form; and it would be an equal mistake to suppose, that in all society of lower caste there is either a want of true refinement or an envy and distrust of all that is above it; but it is also true that there is a magic circle known as "genteel," and a perpetual antagonism prevails here between those who are within and those who desire admittance, but are refused; as there are literary circles where contentions and envyings arise between pedantic scholarship and assuming ignorance.

The ill-breeding so often complained of in the intercourse between the different classes of society, and by none more indignantly than those who exercise it most, results from the factitious value set upon the externals of life by those who estimate them in proportion as they give distinction among men, and not as they increase the means of happiness and usefulness in this world, and so prepare us for the usefulness and happiness of the world to come.

Those among the poor, the ignorant, and the vulgar, whose hearts are burning with envy and hatred; and those among the rich, the learned, and the fashionable, who are rendered arrogant and supercilious by their possessions, are alike unconscious of the true worth of the blessings that excite the covetousness of the one class and the exultation of the other. Each party values man for his possessions, and not for the use that he makes of them; for what he has, and not for what he is. Where this is the case, mutual aversion ultimating itself on both sides in acts of discourtesy, will ever keep alive a spirit of antagonism among the various classes of society; and this will disappear in proportion as society becomes sufficiently Christianized to perceive and acknowledge that every human being is worthy of respect so far as he fulfils the duties of his station; and that we cannot be discourteous even towards the evil and the unfaithful, without indulging feelings of pride and disdain that are incompatible with Christian meekness.

In the social intercourse of equals, and in domestic life, ill-temper, selfishness, and indifference, which is a negative form of selfishness, are the principal sources of ill-breeding. Where the external forms of courtesy are not observed in the family circle, we are almost sure to find perpetually recurring contention and bickering. Rudeness is a constant source of irritation; because, however little the members of a family regard politeness, each will have his own way of being rude, and each will probably be disgusted or angry at some portion of the ill-breeding of all the rest. Rudeness is always angular, and its sharp corners produce discomfort whenever they come in contact with a neighbor. Politeness presents only polished surfaces, and not only never intrudes itself upon a neighbor, but is rarely obtruded upon; for there is no way so effectual of disarming rudeness as by meeting it with thorough politeness; for the rude man can fight only with his own weapons.

Indifference of Manner exhibits a disregard for the comfort and pleasure of those around us, which, though not so obtrusive as rudeness, shows an egotism of disposition incompatible with brotherly love. If we love our neighbor as ourself, we cannot habitually forget his existence so far as to annoy him by neglecting to perform, the common courtesies of life towards him, or interfere with what he is doing by not perceiving that we are in his way.

If we would be thoroughly well-bred, we must be so constantly. It is not very difficult to distinguish in society between those whose manners are assumed for the occasion and those who wear them habitually. The former are apt to forget themselves occasionally, or they overact their part, or if they succeed in sustaining a perfect elegance of deportment that is really pleasing as an effort of art, they always want the grace of naturalness and simplicity which belongs to the Manners of those who have made courtesy and refinement their own by loving them. It is only when we act as we love to act, that our Manners are truly our own. If we cultivate the external forms of politeness from an indirect motive, that is, from the love of approbation, or from pride of character, it is the reward we love, and not the virtue; and if we gain this reward, it is only external and perishable; and is of no benefit to our character, but the reverse, for it ministers only to our pride. If, on the contrary, we cultivate politeness with simplicity, because we believe it to be a virtue, and love it for its own sake, we are sure of the reward of an added grace of character, which can never be taken from us, because it is a part of ourselves; and though we may enjoy the external rewards if they come, we shall not be disturbed if they do not; because these were not the motives that induced our efforts.

Politeness, where it is loved and cultivated with simplicity for its own sake, gives a repose and ease of action to the moral being which may be compared to the comfort and satisfaction resulting to the physical frame from habits of personal cleanliness. The moral tone is elevated and refined by the one, as the animal functions are purified and renewed by the other.

As in civil life liberty to the whole results from the subjection of the evil passions of all to legal enactments, so in social life every individual is free and at ease in proportion as all the rest are subject to the laws of courtesy. Ease and freedom are the result of order, and it is as incorrect to call rude Manners free and easy, as to call licentiousness liberty. No man is truly free who allows his sphere of life to impinge upon that of his neighbor. Fluids are said to move easily because each particle is without angular projections that prevent it from gliding smoothly with or by its companions; and in like manner the ease of society depends on the polish of each individual. If the units of society seek their own selfish indulgence, without regard to the rights of the neighbor, the whole must form a mass of grating atoms in which no one can be free, or at ease.

Indifference, ill-temper, selfishness, envy and arrogance, all positive vices, are the characteristics that ultimate themselves in ill-manners. Rudeness is, as it were, the offensive odor exhaled from the corrupt fruit of an evil tree; and he who would be a branch of the true vine must remember, whenever he is tempted to do a rude thing, that he will never yield to such temptation unless there is hidden somewhere upon his branch fruit that should be cut off and cast into the fire.

The Christian gentleman and lady are such because they love their neighbor as themselves; and to be a thorough Christian without being a gentleman or lady is impossible. Wherever we find the rich without arrogance, and the poor without envy, the various members of society sustaining their mutual relations without suspicion or pretension, the family circle free from rivalry, fault-finding, or discord, we shall find nothing ungentle, for there the spirit of Christianity reigns. He who is pure in heart can never be vulgar in speech, and he who is meek and loving in spirit can never be rude in manner.

COMPANIONSHIP.

Learn to admire rightly; the great pleasure of life is that. Note what the great men admired; they admired great things: narrow spirits admire basely, and worship meanly."

—THACKERAY.

"According to the temper and spirit by which it is influenced, prayer opens or shuts the kingdom of life and peace on the soul of the supplicant, elevating him either to a closer conjunction with the Lord and his angelic kingdom, or plunging him into a more deplorable depth of separation, by immersing him into association with the lost spirits of darkness."

—CLOWES.

* * * * *

Man was not born to live alone, and it is only in and through the relations of the family and the social circle that the better parts of his nature can be developed. Solitude is good occasionally, and they who fly from it entirely can hardly attain to any high degree of spiritual growth; but still in all useful solitude there must be a recognition of some being beside self. He who turns to solitude only to brood over thoughts of self, soon becomes a morbid egoist, and it is only when we study in solitude in order to make our social life more wise and true that our solitary hours are blessed.

Man really alone is something we can hardly imagine. He becomes cognizable almost entirely through his relations with God and with his fellow-men. Heathen philosophy sought to make man wise by withdrawing him from the passions and affections that move him when associated with his fellow-men, in order that he might devote himself to the study of abstract truth. Christian philosophy teaches that truth owes its sanctity to the Divine Love, which alone gives it Life; and that by leading a life of love we acquire the power of understanding the truth. Philosophy is a dead abstraction until piety and charity fill it with the breath of life.

The offices of piety belong in great part to solitude, and the offices of charity to society; but the principle of Companionship is involved in both; for piety associates us with God as charity associates us with man.

All Companionship involves the idea of both giving and receiving. In the offices of piety, in proportion as we give a worship that is earnest and heartfelt, is the warmth and clearness of the influx of heavenly love and wisdom that we receive. In the offices of charity, our love is warmed and our wisdom enlightened in proportion as we disinterestedly seek the true happiness of those whose lives come within the sphere of our influence, guided, not by blind instinct, but by an enlightened Christianity. Thus the quality and quantity of what we receive from Companionship depends on the quality and quantity of what we give.

There is no surer test of Character than the Companionship we habitually seek; for we always prefer the society of those who administer to our dominant love. Some seek the society of their superiors, others of their equals, and others, again, of their inferiors; and the members of each class are actuated in their choice by very various motives. Thus, among the first class are found the ambitious, who seek their superiors because they fancy themselves elevated by the reflection of the attributes they admire; the proud, who fancy themselves degraded by association with their inferiors; and the humble, who seek to be advanced in goodness, in knowledge, or in refinement through intercourse with those who excel. On the other hand are those who seek their inferiors from the vanity that demands admiration as its daily food, or the pride that feels itself oppressed in the presence of a superior, or the philanthropy that loves to give of its stores to those less endowed than itself. The middle class may be actuated in their choice by the love of sympathy in their pursuits, or by a kind of indolence that is disturbed by whatever differs much from itself. There is less purpose and vitality in this class than in either of the others; but merely a desire to float with the surrounding current, whithersoever it may tend.

The constituents of society are so varied in quality, that it would be very difficult for any one to associate exclusively with a particular class; and it may be doubted if we have a right to seek to do so. The variety in social life is adapted to develop the various qualities of the human soul far more perfectly than they could be if the different classes of humanity were entirely separated in their walks. All should be willing to give as well as to receive, and to this end all should be willing to associate in a spirit of brotherly love with their superiors or their inferiors without any feeling either of servility or of elation. We may seek the society of our superiors in order to enrich ourselves, and that of our inferiors in order to give freely even as we have received; while with our equals we alternately give and receive, for no two persons are so similarly endowed but that each may gain by associating with the other. In truth, whichever way the balance may incline, none ever give without receiving, and none can receive without giving.

No Companionship is wise that does not involve the principle of growth. If the influence of our associates does not make us go forward, it will surely cause us to go backward. If we are not elevated by it, we shall certainly be degraded. Two persons cannot associate and either party remain just as he was before; and if we would find in society an element of growth, we must seek for all that is elevating in whatever circles we move; for it is not confined to any particular circle or class, but waits everywhere for the true seeker.

Blessed are the meek, for they shall inherit the earth, said the Lord, teaching as never man taught; and it is in proportion as we walk meekly with our fellow-men that our capacities become capable of receiving, to their fullest extent, the influx of goodness and truth that should be the end of social intercourse. Nothing obstructs our receptivity so much as that egoism of thought and affection which keeps self perpetually before the mind's eye, and to this egoism meekness is the direct opposite. Meekness implies forgetfulness of self. There is nothing servile about it, but it pursues its way in pure simplicity, forgetting self in its steadfast devotion to what it seeks. Egoism pursues its aims from love of self and of the world, and confides in its own strength for success. Meekness pursues its aims from the love of excellence, and confiding in the strength of the Lord. The first love is dim of sight, and often satisfies itself with the shadow of what it seeks, while its strength is too feeble to grasp the higher forms of excellence. The second love is full of light, because its eye is single; it can be satisfied only with substance, and its endeavors know no limit, because its strength comes from Him who never fails nor wearies.

Meekness is always ready to receive of the excellence it seeks, through whatever medium it can be obtained; while egoism is perpetually hindered in its advancement by its unwillingness to owe it to any source out of self.

Similar results follow in giving as in receiving. Meekness gives in simplicity from love to the neighbor, and feels as great pleasure in imparting from its stores as in receiving additions to them, because the pleasure it imparts is reflected back upon itself, making all its good offices twice blessed. Egoism is twice cursed, as all that it receives and all that it gives perpetually adds to its love of self; for it values what it possesses because it is its own, and imparts to others because it enjoys a feeling of superiority over the recipient of its possessions. Meekness builds itself up; egoism puffs itself up. To meekness Companionship is a perpetual source of healthful growth; while to egoism it furnishes food only to supply the demands of a morbid enlargement, destructive to all manly and womanly symmetry.

Society at large, according as we walk in it in a spirit of meekness or a spirit of egoism, thus serves to develop and expand our powers, or to narrow and degrade them more and more continually. To the casual observer, the difference in the advancement of the two classes may not in early life be apparent. The forth-putting pretension of egoism may indeed cause it to seem the more rapidly advancing character of the two; but the progress of years will widen the separation between their paths, till it shall be seen as a great gulf, of which the opposite sides have naught in common. Advancing age will show the egoist narrow-minded and overbearing, peevish and fault-finding; while he who pursues his even course, walking in Christian meekness with his fellow-men, will in old age exhibit ever-enlarging charity and ever-expanding wisdom, and his gray hairs will seem like a crown of glory.

It may seem almost needless to speak of the danger to Character that is involved in seeking the Companionship of the worthless or the evil- disposed. "Can one handle pitch and not be defiled?" Yet the usages of society are so disordered, that the possession of wealth, family distinction, or personal elegance, though accompanied by ignorance, folly, or even dissoluteness, is sometimes a surer passport into what is termed good society than the best culture of mind and heart, where external advantages have been denied.

When we value mankind according to their external advantages, our moral standard is as false as the drawing upon a Chinese plate. We have no true moral perspective. Our ideas of right and wrong are confused and imperfect, and in danger of becoming corrupt. We laugh at the stupidity of the poor Chinaman in his attempts after beauty in art, while in morals we are quite as stupid as he. Believing ourselves wise, we are fools. It is very hard to escape being unduly influenced by the opinions of society; but the more earnestly we seek true excellence for ourselves, the more easily we learn to value true excellence in others, and, to overlook the opinions of the world. The more independent we become of opinion, the better will be the influence we exert upon society, as well as that which we receive from it in return.

If the influence of our Companionship with those whom we meet in general society and in the daily avocations of life be important, far more so is that which comes to us through the friends whom we select from the world at large as best adapted to minister to our happiness; and in proportion as they are near and dear to us will their influence be strong and deep.

The choice of friends is influenced by an equal variety of motives, and of a similar nature as those that lead to the selection of the social circle. There is often no better foundation than selfishness for what passes current in the world for ardent friendship. The selfish and worldly love from selfish and worldly motives, and doubtless they receive their reward; but if we would derive the advantages to Character that result from a wise Companionship, we must select our friends without undue regard to the opinions of the world, and impelled by a desire for moral or intellectual advancement. Falsehood and fickleness in friendship result from its being built upon merely selfish or circumstantial foundations. When built upon mutual respect and affection, it contains no element of decay or change; and they who trust to any other foundation have no right to complain if their confidence is abused and disappointed.

Persons sometimes suppose themselves the fast friends of others, when their affection is merely the result of benefits received directly or indirectly; and if these benefits are withheld, their supposed friendship is dissipated at once, or perhaps changed to enmity. Such a friendship is merely circumstantial, and has no just claim to the name. Mere juxtaposition, the habit of seeing each other every day, is often sufficient to produce what the parties concerned esteem friendship, and to occasion the freest interchange of confidence. The slightest change of circumstance, a few miles of separation, an inadvertent offence, a trival difference of opinion, a clashing of interests, are, any one of them, sufficient to bring such an intimacy to an end, and to cast reproach upon the sacred name of friendship, when friendship had never existed between the parties for a single moment.

Genuine friendship can exist only between persons of some elevation of moral character, and its strength and devotion will be commensurate with the degree of this moral elevation.

Truthfulness, frankness, disinterestedness, and faithfulness are qualities absolutely essential to friendship, and these must be crowned by a sympathy that enters into all the joys, the sorrows, and the interests of the friend, that delights in all his upward progress, and, when he stumbles or falls, as all at times must, stretches out the helping hand, not condescendingly nor scornfully, but in the simplicity of true charity, that forgives even as it would be forgiven, and is tender and patient even where it condemns. In such a friendship there is no room for rivalry, weariness, distrust, or anything subversive of confidence. With the selfish and the worldly, such a connection cannot exist, because with them rivalries and clashing interests must arise; for it is only among the seekers after excellence that there is room for the gratification of the desires of all. Neither can it exist between the false, for falsehood shuts the door upon confidence; nor with the morally weak, the foolish, or the idle, for they weary of each other even as they weary of themselves.

Of all earthly Companionship, there is none so deeply fraught with weal or woe, with blessing or with cursing, as the Companionship of married life. After this relationship is formed, although the threads still remain the same, the whole warp and woof of the being are dyed with a new color, woven according to a new pattern. Character is never the same after marriage as before. There is a new impetus given by it to the powers of thought and affection, inducing them to a different activity, and deciding what tendencies are henceforth to take the lead in the action of the mind; whether the soul is to spread its wings for a higher flight than it has hitherto ventured, or to sit with closed pinions, content to be of the earth, earthy. All are interested, even strangers, In hearing of the establishment of a newly married pair in what relates to the equipage of external life. Far more interesting would it be if we could trace the mental establishing that is going on, as old traits of character are confirmed or cast aside, and new ones developed or implanted.

This union, so sacred that it even supersedes that which exists between parent and child, should be entered upon only from the highest and purest motives; and then, let worldly prosperity come or go as it may, this twain whom God has joined, not by a mere formal ritual of the Church, but by a true spiritual union that man cannot put asunder, are a heaven unto themselves, and peace will ever dwell within their habitation.

In proportion as a true marriage of the affections between the pure in heart is productive of the highest happiness that can exist on earth, so every remove from it diminishes the degree of this happiness until it passes into the opposite, and becomes, in its most worldly and selfish form, a fountain of misery, of a quality absolutely infernal.

Amid the disorder and imperfection reigning in the world, it is not to be supposed that a large proportion of marriages should be truly heavenly. In order to arrive at this, both parties must be of a higher moral standing than is often reached at an age when marriage is usually entered upon; but unless the character of each is inclined heavenward there is no rational ground for anticipating happiness, except of the lowest kind.

Many persons of a naturally amiable disposition enjoy what may seem a high degree of happiness, through their sympathy with each other in worldliness and ambition; but such happiness is not of a kind that can endure the clouds and tempests of life. It is nourished only by the good things of this world, and, if it cannot obtain them, is converted into the greater wretchedness because the being who is dearest in life shares this wretchedness. When, on the contrary, things heavenly are those most highly prized and earnestly sought, each party helps to sustain the other in all earthly privations and disappointments; for each is looking beyond and above the trials of earth, and each is in possession of a hope, nay, a fruition, that cannot be taken away, and which is dearer than all that is lost. With them, to suffer together is to rob suffering of half its weight, and almost all its bitterness. Whatever earthly deprivation may befall them, the kingdom of heaven is ever within their souls.

The Companionship of our fellow-beings is not confined to the living men and women around us, but comes to us, through books, from all nations and ages. Wise teachers stand ever ready to instruct us, gentle moralists to console and strengthen us, poets to delight us. Scarce a country village is so poor that there may not be found beneath its roofs the printed words of more great men than ever lived at any one period of the earth's history.

We are too apt to use books, as well as society, merely for our amusement; to read the books that chance to fall into our hands, or to associate with the persons we happen to meet with, and not stop to ask ourselves if nothing better is within our reach. It may not be in our power to associate with great living minds, but the mental wealth of the past is within the reach of all. We boast much that we are a reading people, but it may be well to inquire how intelligently we read. The catalogues of books borrowed from our public libraries show, that, where the readers of works of amusement are counted by hundreds, the readers of instructive books are numbered by units. In conversation, it is not uncommon to hear persons expressing indifference or dislike to whole classes of books,—to hear Travels denounced as stupid, Biography as tame, and History as heavy and dull. It does not seem to occur to the mass of minds that any purpose beyond the amusement of the moment is to be thought of in reading, or that any plan should be laid, or any principles adopted, in the choice of books to be read.

It is undoubtedly a great good that nearly all our people are taught to read, but it is a small fraction of the community that reads to much good purpose. Children, so soon as they have acquired the use of the alphabet, are inundated with little juvenile stories, some of them good, but most of them silly, and many vulgar. As they grow older, successions of similar works of fiction await them, until they arrive at adolescence, when they are fully prepared for all the wealth of folly, vulgarity, falsehood, and wickedness that is bound up within the yellow covers of most of the cheap novels that infest every highway of the nation.

As you are jostled through the streets of our populous cities, or take your seat in a crowded railway-car, you are, perhaps, impressed with the general air of rudeness that pervades the scene,—a rudeness of a kind so new to the world, that, no old word sufficing to describe it, a new name has been coined, and the swaggering, careless, sensual looking beings, reeking with the fumes of tobacco, that make up the masses of our moving population, are adequately described only by the word *rowdy*. As yet, no title has been found for the female of this class, —bold, dashing, loud-talking and loud-laughing, ignorant, vain, and so coarse that she supposes fine clothes and assuming manners are all that is necessary to elevate her to the rank of a lady. Perhaps you wonder how so numerous a race of these beings has come to exist; but that boy at your elbow, bending under the weight of his literary burden, is a colporteur for converting the men and women of this "enlightened nation" to rowdyism. Those books portray just such men and women as you see before you, and that is why they are welcomed so warmly. A few cents will buy from that boy enough folly and impurity to gorge a human mind for a week, and possibly few among this throng often taste more wholesome intellectual food.

It is probable that some of these persons are the children of intelligent and well-bred parents; but their fathers were engrossed in business, and their mothers in family cares, and thought they had no time to form the moral and intellectual tastes of the immortal minds committed to their charge. They fancied that if they sent their children to good schools, and provided liberally for all their external wants, they had done enough. Ignorant nursery maids, perhaps, taught them morals and manners, while the father toiled to accumulate the means for supplying their external wants, and the mother hemmed ruffles and scolloped trimming to make people say, "How *sweetly* those children are dressed!" as the maid paraded them through the streets, teaching them their first lessons in vulgar vanity.

A child may be educated at the best schools without acquiring any taste for good literature. The way a parent treats a child in relation to its books has far more influence in this respect than a teacher can possibly possess. A mother, even if she is not an educated woman, can learn to read understandingly, and can

146

teach her child to read in the same way. She can talk to it about its books, and awaken a desire in its mind to understand what it reads. Children are always curious in regard to the phenomena of nature, and whether this curiosity lives or dies depends very much on the answers it receives to its first questions. If the mother cannot answer them herself, she can help the child to find an answer somewhere else, and she should beware how she deceives herself with the idea that she has not time to attend to the moral and intellectual wants of her child. She has no right to so immerse all her own mind in the cares of life that she cannot, while attending to them, talk rationally with her children. The mothers who best fulfil their higher duties towards their children are quite as often found among those who are compelled to almost constant industry of the hands, as among those of abundant leisure. There is nothing in the handiwork of the housekeeper or the seamstress that need absorb all the mental attention; and hers must be an ill-regulated mind that cannot ply the needle, or perform the more active duties of the household, and yet listen to the child as it reads its little books, and converse with it about the moral lessons or the intellectual instruction they contain. The mother has it in her power to influence the mode in which the child makes companions of its books more than any other person; and the character of its Companionship with them through life will generally depend in a great degree on the tastes and habits acquired in childhood.

Many parents who guard their children with jealous care from the contamination of rude and vicious society among other children, allow them to associate with ideal companions of a very degraded kind. The parent should check the propensity, not only to read bad books, but also to read idle or foolish books, by exciting the action of the mind towards something better. Merely to deny improper books is not enough. Something must be given in place of them, or the craving will continue, and the child will be very apt to gratify its appetite in secret.

Children are easily led to observe nature, animate or inanimate, with interest, and there are many simple books

147

illustrating the departments of natural science which mothers could make interesting to their children at the same time that they instructed themselves. Juvenile works on history abound, and through them the child may be led, as intelligence expands, to seek more extended and thorough treatises; and the sympathy of the mother should be ready to help him on his way. It is mere self-deception in those mothers who deny their mental capacity, or their command of time, to aid their children in their mental progress. It is a *moral* want of their own, far more than everything else, that causes them to shrink from this most important responsibility.

Those who have passed the period of childhood, who have taken upon themselves the responsibility of all that concerns their own minds, and who have any desire after upward progress, should remember that the books they love best are those which reflect their own characteristics. Every one looks up to his favorite books, and the tone of his mind is influenced by them in consequence. In our Companionship with our fellow- beings we may be governed to a great extent by our desire to stand well with the world, and therefore seek the society of those whom the world most admires rather than those we most enjoy. In the choice of our books there is much less influence of this kind exerted upon us. In the retirement of our homes we may daily consort with the low or the wicked, as they are delineated in books, and our standing with the world be in no way affected, while the poison we imbibe will work all the more surely that it works secretly. They whose ideas of right and wrong are dependent on the judgment of the world may need even this poor guide, and suffer from the want of it; for in doing what the world does not know, and therefore cannot condemn, they may encounter evil and danger from which even the love of the world would protect them, if the same things were to be exposed to the public eye. We have no more moral right to read bad books than to associate with bad men, and it would be well for us in selecting our books to be governed by much the same principles as in the selection of our associates; to feel that they are, in fact, companions and friends whose opinions cannot fail to exert a powerful influence upon us, and that we cannot associate with them indiscriminately without great danger to our characters.

The Book of books, the Word of God, should occupy the first place in our estimation; and the test question in regard to the value of all other books is, whether they draw us towards, or away from, the Bible. So far as they are written with a genuine love for goodness and truth, books in every department of science and literature have a tendency, more or less strong, to increase our reverence and love for the Source of all goodness and truth; and no book can be subversive of our faith in the Scriptures that has not its foundation laid in falsehood.

Nature may tell us of a Creator, but the Bible alone reveals a Father. Nature describes him as far from us, removed beyond all sympathy, before whose power we tremble, and whose mercy we might strive to propitiate by sacrifices or entreaties; but from the Bible we learn that he is near at hand, watching every pulsation of the heart, listening to every aspiration that we breathe; that we walk with him so long as we obey his commandments, and that though we may turn from him, he never turns from us; that when we approach him in prayer, it should not be with fear, but with love; and loving him with the knowledge that he first loved us, we find that prayer, in its true form, is a Companionship, and that the Father rejoices over his child in proportion as the child rejoices in approaching the throne of mercy.

Pure and holy influences come to us immediately through our Companionship with those among our fellow-beings who have received of the overflowings of the Divine Fountain of goodness and truth. But when we reverently approach that Fountain, we receive immediately, with a power and fulness that can descend upon us through no human being.

What we receive through other mediums reaches only the lower and more external planes of our being; but prayer brings us, if we pray aright, before the throne of the Most High, and opens those inmost chambers of the soul that remain for ever closed and empty unless they are opened and filled by the immediate presence of the Lord. These constitute that Holy of Holies which is the inmost of every human soul. The world at large may enter its outer courts, chosen friends may minister before the altar of its sanctuary, but within all this there is a holier place, which none but the Lord can enter; for it is the seat of the vital principle of the soul, which can be touched and quickened by no hand but his.

The quality of the life of the whole being depends upon the degree in which we suffer the Lord to dwell within our souls. His Companionship fills and vivifies everything that is below it. The more entirely we walk with the Lord, the more constant we shall be in the performance of all our duties. The more entirely we open our hearts to his influence, the more benefit we shall receive from all other influences. The more reverently we listen to the truth that comes directly from him, the more capable we shall be of finding out and appreciating the truth that comes indirectly. The more we open our hearts to receive his love, the more perfect will be the love we shall bear towards our fellow-beings. The more constantly we feel that we are in his presence, the more perfect will be the hourly outgoings of our lives.

Intimate Companionship with the Lord does not abstract us from the world around us, but fills that world with new meanings. There is nothing abstract in the nature of the Deity. He is operating perpetually upon all nature. Gravity, organic life, instinct, human thought and affection, are forms of his influx manifesting itself in varying relations. Wherever he comes there is life, and his activity knows no end.

Let no human being think that he holds Companionship with the Lord, because he loves to retire apart, to pray, or to contemplate the divine attributes, if, at such times, he looks down upon, and shuns the haunts of men. The bigot may do so; and all his thoughts about things holy, all his prayers, only confirm him in his spiritual pride. Every thought of self-elevation, every feeling that tends towards "I am holier than thou," smothers the breath of all true prayer, and associates us with the spirit of evil; for our prayers cannot be blessed to us if pride inspire them. Neither let any one suppose himself spiritual because material life or material duties oppress him. God made the material world as a school for his children; and he will not keep us here a moment after we are prepared for a higher state. We are putting ourselves back when we work impatiently, in the feeling that the duties of life are beneath us.

If we would abide with our Heavenly Father, we must cooperate with him perpetually. It is doing his will, not contemplating it, that teaches us his attributes, and builds us up in his image and likeness. His fields are ever white unto the harvest; let us work while it is yet day, ever bearing in mind that he gives us the power to work, and that we can work rightly only so long as we live in the constant acknowledgment of our dependence upon Him.

THE END.

www.ingramcontent.com/pod-product-compliance
Lightning Source LLC
Chambersburg PA
CBHW070805290326
41931CB00011BA/2139